Augsburg College
George Sverdrup Library
Minneapolis, Minnesota 55404

PUBLIC SERVICE IN
GREAT BRITAIN

The University of North Carolina Press, Chapel Hill, N. C.; The Baker and Taylor Company, New York; Oxford University Press, London; Maruzen-Kabushiki-Kaisha, Tokyo; Edward Evans & Sons, Ltd., Shanghai; D. B. Centen's Wetenschappelijke Boekhandel, Amsterdam.

Public Service
IN GREAT BRITAIN

By HIRAM MILLER STOUT

With an introduction by
W. Y. ELLIOTT

CHAPEL HILL
THE UNIVERSITY OF NORTH CAROLINA PRESS
1938

COPYRIGHT, 1938, BY
THE UNIVERSITY OF NORTH CAROLINA PRESS

MANUFACTURED IN THE UNITED STATES OF AMERICA
Van Rees Press, New York

TO

CAROLINE

PREFACE

Lord Tweedsmuir, the Governor-General of Canada, said on a recent occasion, "I think that Britain can offer to the Commonwealth, and indeed to the whole world, one example which has a true spiritual value—the example of a closely integrated people among whom unselfish public service is still regarded as a supreme duty and privilege."

The value of such an example increases daily as governments expand their areas of activity. Everywhere peoples are faced with the problem of selecting and training men equal to the enormous responsibilities of thinking, planning, and administering for the public weal.

While no complete solution for this problem has been found in England, the British have established ideals of public service which have raised their political institutions to recognized high levels. It is the purpose of this book to examine the development and present-day application of these ideals in two important fields of public service—the national Civil Service and Parliament.

An attempt has been made to present within a reasonable compass a description of the personnel of these institutions and their relationships to one another and to the public. The effort to treat the subject in a manner of interest and of service to the general student of government has involved some sacrifice of detail. However, it is hoped that the reader may be introduced to the traditions, conditions of service, and ideals of the people who in large part shape the destinies of Great Britain, and with it much of the modern world.

In the collection of material for this book and in its writing the author has become indebted to many people. A number of persons in official life in Great Britain generously contributed time and information. It is not possible to mention them all by name, but I wish to thank Sir Warren Fisher and Sir James Rae who were especially helpful. Other civil servants, the secretaries of staff associations, and several people in academic life in England offered advice and suggestions which aided greatly in the writing of various chapters of the book.

Professor Elliott's offer to write an introduction to the book was only one of his many kindnesses. My thanks are also due the Harvard Committee for Research in the Social Sciences for the financial aid it made available. My former colleague at DePauw University, Professor Harold Zink, gave generously of his time in reading and criticizing the manuscript, and my friend, Alvin J. Rockwell, made helpful suggestions.

I am appreciative of the willingness of several publishers to permit quotation from books published by them.

Hiram Miller Stout

Contents

	PAGE
PREFACE	vii
INTRODUCTION BY W. Y. ELLIOTT	xi

CHAPTER

I. THE CLASSES AND THE MASSES IN POLITICS . . 1

II. THE OLD OFFICIALDOM AND ITS REFORM . . . 16
Parliament—The Civil Service: The Beginning of Reform—The Development of the Civil Service

III. THE HONORABLE MEMBER 59

IV. THE PERMANENT BRAIN TRUST 77

V. THE ADMINISTRATIVE ARMY 114

VI. THE CIVIL SERVICE AND THE PUBLIC 135

VII. MASTERS AND SERVANTS 156

APPENDIX 177

BIBLIOGRAPHY 181

INDEX 185

INTRODUCTION

By W. Y. Elliott

A BOOK ON THE PUBLIC SERVICE in Great Britain runs the risk of covering very well-known ground. Alternatively, if it attempts to pursue rather special inquiries it loses its usefulness to the general student. The great merit of Dr. Stout's study is that it shows the evolution of government in England over the last hundred years or more in a fresh and, at the same time, a lucid, simple focus. He has chosen the Civil Service as the central point of his inquiry, but he has never lost sight of the relations of the Civil Service to public policy and to the control of public policy by Parliament.

There is a tag from Benjamin Franklin which in these days of emphasis on public administration is often quoted: "Governments are like clocks—as they are made by men so may they be marred and ruined." It is with this definite insight that Dr. Stout has shown the relation of public servants, both in the Civil Service and in Parliament, to the realities of British government. No student of politics today any longer has doubts as to the necessity of securing a responsible bureaucracy if the modern state is to function under democratic control. England is ordinarily held up to the world as having most successfully solved that problem. It is a matter of general agreement that the British Civil Service has escaped the rigidities of method that characterize both the French and the German services and that it has recruited, through the system explained by Dr. Stout, as able a group of administrators as any modern government can boast today.

If this impression is not erroneous, the reasons which lie behind the superiority of the British Service as an instrument for the modern state are exceedingly important to students of politics. It is not simply a question of the choice of the right man by proper methods of selection but of opening up a career to the talented and of making those talents effective. That implies that the Parliamentary machinery and the membership of the controlling representative body and the Cabinet should be of such a character as to use the instrument that is provided to them. It is precisely in seeing this relationship between the Civil Service and the Cabinet member and the Parliamentarian that the present work ought to be most valuable.

I count it a positive virtue that so many public documents and so many rather inaccessible memoirs should have been made available to students in a single book. There is to my knowledge no other contemporary work on the British Civil Service that covers anything like this range. The perspective which Dr. Stout has achieved on problems of promotion, recruitment, and administrative syndicalism in relation to Treasury control is really remarkable for anyone who is not steeped in the British tradition by birth and upbringing. His very valuable contacts from Sir Warren Fisher down to the bemedaled doormen of the Home Office or the India Office have all helped him to interpret, as few American students have succeeded in doing, the spirit of the Civil Service.

It is difficult to put into a formal text the kind of feeling that sometimes shows through even satires on the Civil Service such as Trollope's *Three Clerks* or Georges Courteline's immortal French satire, *Messieurs Les Ronds-du-Cuir*. The flavor of a civil service which gives it a peculiar character is possibly only to be appreciated through a literary treatment in the form of a novel or a drama. It is well nigh impossible to reproduce the stodgy security that is the very atmosphere of, say, the Colonial Office. Tea, served in the offices, breaks the long routine of the afternoon. The endless corridors stuffed with old files echo to steps never too hurried. The low interchange of the gossipy bits among the clerks at work in the library reveal the foibles of their superiors. In the lift going home from the day's work they make solemn arrangements for the social activities of the civil servants' associations. All these things give a feeling, unconveyable by blue books or documents, of orderly routine and an accepted way of life! The peculiar texture of English life which makes such admirable but demanding domestic servants affects also public servants. There is a sense of "my station and its duties" that runs very deep in the well-organized traditionalism of a country that enjoyed both the prestige and the tranquillity of Victoria's long reign.

It may be that this smug assurance, that things will always go on being much as they have been, makes the British too little critical of their own machinery. They seem to feel that though other empires fall, Britannia remains. Lack of imagination may prove to be the gravest handicap to the British governing minds in a period such as the one in which we are living. That the phlegmatic British have decided advantages of morale under the severest test that crisis can afford, we have adequate proof from the experience of the last war. But the efforts which seem necessary to avoid the disintegration of a world system may well fail to come from a public so accustomed to security in all its aspects as the well-governed British public has grown to be.

Though this psychological aspect of politics lies somewhat beyond the scope of Dr. Stout's analysis, he gives one, in his well-chosen excerpts and quotations, the best material for constructing a picture of the Civil Service at work. He is acutely conscious—and he shows it throughout —that the modern state, even where it is striving most to escape becoming totalitarian, must necessarily undertake a range of direct and indirect control over economic and social life that makes it the regulating mechanism of all society. Surely it is this fact that explains the modern preoccupation with religions of state rather than of the other world. The present is a period of myth-making in terms of hero worship and the re-enthroning of the Caesars.

If the democracies are to escape this trend, they must be able to create instruments of government that can govern. The frustration of the demands for social security today, with the accompanying pressures toward rearmament in terms of national survival, push every government toward more and more centralization and planning. It is abundantly clear from experience that planning even the conditions of an economy through the budget, through the control of banking and credit, through government regulation of utilities and natural resources, through public works, relief, and social insurance—all these universally accepted necessities of the democratic state require a civil service adequate to its task. For it is the civil servant who is the channel of actual contact between the thing called "government" and us who are governed. Unless the civil servant is capable of exercising administrative discretion without the arbitrary abuse of his powers, bureaucracy becomes "The New Despotism," as the Chief Justice, Lord Hewart, has called it.

This delegation of legislative powers to the civil servant, in spite of every judicial protest in this country and in England, must continue as the duties of government increase and as the range of contacts with individual life becomes greater and more complicated. It is impossible for a body like Congress or Parliament to direct the life of a great modern nation through legislative detail. In this country we have attempted to devolve upon the so-called independent regulatory commissions a great mass of rule-making. In Great Britain the more frequent channel is the government department since the British Parliament maintains its responsible control over the bureaucracy through ministers chosen from its own ranks.

Just as today in the United States there is developing a hue and cry against the commission form of government on the grounds that it confuses in a single body the functions of prosecutor, lawmaker, and judge, so in England there is a grave concern about the increased legislative powers that are exercised with no effective Parliamentary scrutiny by government departments. The Ministry of Health or the Office of the Home Secretary today exercises a range of control over the lives of individuals in England which would be capable of very serious arbitrary abuses. Fortunately Parliament is still a sounding board which is extremely sensitive to any such usurpation of powers or abuses of discretion. Dr. Stout's inquiry into the membership of Parliament and the nature of public careers perhaps does not do full justice in this respect to the personal sort of relationship that the constituent feels exists between every Englishman and his member of Parliament. Protests are effective, because the member likes to pose as the champion of his constituents.

The reasons for this are not far to seek. Parliament has on the whole become more and more a body of critics rather than a board of directors. The major decisions of general policy are now delegated by Parliament to the Cabinet so completely that the party system exercises only in very large terms the shaping of policy through Parliament. The result is that the member of Parliament becomes increasingly interested in performing his rôle as a spokesman for his constituents and as a critic. Even members of the "government" back benches, normally well disciplined in partisan support of the Cabinet, take the greatest delight in embarrassing a government department which seems to have overstepped the bonds of traditional English respect for civil liberties. Perhaps that is why the "Report of the Committee on Ministers' Powers," which suggested making more effective the control of the House of Commons over the powers exercised by Ministers, has not yet been implemented in one very important respect. There is as yet little change indicated in the procedure of the House of Commons looking toward the organization of a special committee to scrutinize delegated legislation. Apparently in fact the abuses were not so serious as critics allege, or alternatively the remedies were felt to be more adequate through the ordinary channels of questions in the House of Commons or letters to *The Times,* etc.

While it is certainly true that the rearmament program and the drawing together of England in crisis have reduced the critical rôle of Parliament and increased the area within which governmental departments are free to operate without much check, it is far from being true that England is today a Fascist state or anything like one. The essence of Fascism is the repression of criticism by governmental agencies or by an organized party with terrorist methods. Fortunately in England today criticism can be heard not only in the Halls of Parliament but from the ranks of the civil servants themselves.

The well-known story of a crusty old official in the Home Office is a case in point. His Minister at a meeting of a Cabinet committee was producing a policy which ran counter to the whole experience of the Home Office and which threatened grave possibilities in the judgment of some of his other Cabinet colleagues. The privileged official, whose loyalty and discretion could not be questioned in the light of long service, finally interrupted decisively with a rather unexpected question: "When are you going to stop being such a . . . fool?" The effect was as decisive as it was overwhelming and provoked an uproar of laughter which settled the issue out of hand. The civil servant became shortly after a governor of an Indian province, showing that his forthrightness commanded appreciation rather than condemnation.

The very essence of the relations between civil servants and politicians in England is that of the mutual dependence of the two. The civil servant knows perfectly well that he cannot hope to put across his own particular ideas or those of his department without persuading the politician of their soundness. On the other hand, the politician

INTRODUCTION xvii

knows how many serious mistakes he has been saved from making by listening to the detached criticism of the permanent officials. He is conscious that his ability to meet a highly critical Opposition is dependent very largely upon the loyal support and the documentation furnished him by his own aides.[1] There results one of the most natural "give and takes" that political teamwork in England displays, and there are many of them. Cabinet solidarity—that much vaunted central arch of the British system—is a less important thing than intradepartmental solidarity, in terms of morale. Occasionally there are, of course, disastrous Ministers, and once in a while there are civil servants who, though not quite disastrous enough to be dismissed, are a dead loss to the Service. But this is very rare in a system in which competition both for the permanent offices and for ministerial posts is extremely severe.

One must remember that the British Parliament is rather like an English public school as described in *Tom Brown's School Days*. The whole school divides into two sides for a game, and the leaders of each side, chosen by a sort of natural selection, direct strategy. In Parliament, the better side, as tested in terms of a general election and the

[1] There was one amusing instance that I witnessed, in which a Cabinet Minister in answer to a question in the House of Commons began reading off statistics from the wrong memorandum to the utter consternation of the permanent official who was watching his Chief from just outside the sacred circle of the members of the House of Commons. The antics of the agitated permanent official in attempting to get the attention of his Chief convulsed the House and drew their attention to the spectacle that the Minister was making of himself. Finally the assistant secretary in desperation weighted a note with change that he had in his pocket and threw it up to the desk just under the Speaker's chair, thus attracting the attention of his Chief. The look of horror that went over the face of the Minister when he read the contents of the note must have been indicative of what was in it, but he immediately regained his composure and calmly explained his mistake. An opposition member was unkind enough to raise a point of order with the Speaker as to whether or not Ministers were entitled to outside aid in the course of a speech in the House of Commons. Though the question raised a laugh, it raised nothing more, as every member of the House knew how much in the hands of his permanent officials their Ministers were.

confidence of the country, is finally selected to compete against foreign teams. This perpetual scrimmaging on the whole playing field, in theory at least, serves to keep the team fit and up to its responsibility for defending the national interest.

Today there are some questions about the adequacy of this traditional machinery. In the first place, as Dr. Stout has shown, under war-time conditions it proved to be necessary to create a small imperial war cabinet of the Prime Minister and five or six other members who could make all the decisions of high policy, calling in their other colleagues only for special consultation. This tendency toward working out something like a general staff within the British Government did not stop with the Armistice. In matters of high policy since the War, as Mr. Ivor Jennings has noted in his useful work on *Cabinet Government,* control has been generally transferred to the Committee on Imperial Defense. There is a strong trend today in England to shift the collective responsibility of the inner Cabinet once more, as during the War, to a group around the Prime Minister, a group whose departmental and administrative duties are rendered as little onerous as possible.

This approximation of a sort of directing general staff has been further increased in its effectiveness by putting a permanent general staff at its disposal through the Cabinet Office—also a creature of the War.[2] This office is, properly speaking, a secretariat headed by Sir Maurice Hankey, who is also—note well—the Clerk of the Privy Council and the Secretary of the Committee of Imperial Defense. Sir Maurice Hankey studiously gives out the impression that he has nothing whatever to do with policy

[2] The same preoccupation appears in the Report of the President's Committee on Administrative Management (the so-called Brownlow Report), particularly in the sections dealing with the secretariat of the President and the regrouping of the departments. The obvious model for this report has been the Haldane Commission on the Machinery of Government in Great Britain (1918).

INTRODUCTION xix

and is merely a sort of clearing house for all the departmental relations that require Cabinet attention. Yet many of the students of the British system shrewdly suspect that where imperial interests are affected and in matters of high policy, especially of rearmament, Sir Maurice Hankey's decisions or influence may be quite as important as that of the Permanent Under-Secretary of the Foreign Office—until recently Sir Robert Vansittart, now Sir Alexander Cadogan—or even that of the Permanent Secretary of the Treasury, Sir Warren Fisher. There are others who would go so far as to say that where these three officials are in agreement, Cabinet policy may be taken already to have been formed. That is undoubtedly both an exaggeration and a mistake since these three officials would hardly be likely to be in agreement on any but the most general lines and on obvious matters. More than that, undoubtedly they would be extremely chary of expressing any opinion at all. But there is this much truth in the suspicion, that the attitude of the permanent Civil Service which filters up to these heads through all the channels of minutes and consultations is a most effective factor in all British policy, foreign and domestic.

There remains for consideration one other aspect of the charge that "bureaucracy triumphant" is destroying the old safeguards of the "rule of law" in England. Many lawyers, like C. K. Allen, take a very dark view of the tendency in delegated legislation to relieve government departments from scrutiny by the ordinary courts. In this country the American Bar Association has, through its Committee on Administrative Justice, been inclined to the view that we need to create special types of administrative courts for purposes of reviewing the acts of administrative agents, particularly of our regulatory commissions. But it is fair to say that the lawyers in this country rejoice in the additional safeguards of judicial review of all acts of government for constitutionality so that they can be confident of having our regular courts pass upon any issues that the latter may desire to consider. But in England a similar recommendation by Professor W. A. Robson in giving evidence before the Committee on Ministers' Powers was rejected by the Committee in its report. The British who have no such provision as we have for review of legislation and executive acts on constitutional grounds, apparently cherish the recourse to ordinary courts and fear the development of anything like a special branch of administrative law on the French or German models. My opinion is that in this matter Professor Robson was right and that the only possibility of introducing a more adequate judicial restraint is in the creation of more specialized types of administrative tribunals. The alternative of review by the ordinary courts interposes procedural and other delays so great that a sovereign legislature like Parliament is frequently unwilling to have its agents (the Ministers) thus encumbered. One must remember always that the question of "the law's delays" still agitates men. In time of crisis it is apt to be more feared than "the ignorance of office."

One may expect in England, therefore, no recession from the tremendous discretionary powers that have been granted to government departments and, in effect, to the civil servants who man them. On the contrary, every crisis such as that of 1931 and 1932 produces a return to government by decree, in which Parliament becomes very largely a rubber stamp. As the times in which we live are heavy with the atmosphere of crises it is hardly likely that this trend in government will be reversed.

A study such as Dr. Stout's, therefore, which shows in the perspective of official inquiries and unofficial anecdote the true working of the British civil servants in relation to the Parliamentary system is as useful a contribution as a scholar could make today to the understanding of one of the central problems of representative government.

PUBLIC SERVICE IN
GREAT BRITAIN

CHAPTER I

The Classes and the Masses in Politics

IT IS A COMMONPLACE that throughout the whole Western world there has been a vast enlargement of the area of government during the past fifty years. The old laissez-faire doctrine, having freed social, political, and economic systems of remnants of outworn restraints, collapsed before the demands of great populations living in a new mechanical age. The result has been that legislatures have invaded fields formerly left to custom or the so-called free play of social and economic forces and have created administrative machines to supervise, regulate, and control. As one of the leading personalities of this new era, Ramsay MacDonald, once wrote, "Problems of State become more complicated and exacting; whole fields of activity which our fathers regarded as being fenced off from Parliamentary and Whitehall concern have been taken in, and none of the old burdens permanently removed. The public estate has been widened, not a foot has been alienated." [1]

Political theorists may dispute over a name for the new period—modified capitalism, mild socialism, paternalism, or what not—but that involves a good deal of metaphysical hair-splitting that need not detain us. Perhaps it has been evolving too rapidly to enable it to be tagged and catalogued, but at any rate there has been a deviation from the past which escapes the notice of no one who stops to ponder a moment.

In Great Britain this governmental intervention has

[1] J. Ramsay MacDonald, "Politics and Public Life," *The Problem of a Career*, ed. J. A. R. Cairns (London, 1926), p. 101.

taken a number of forms. Some of it is in the shape of outright ownership. Telephones, telegraphs, and radio broadcasting are familiar examples. In other cases it is the provision of various social services, such as old age pensions, health and unemployment insurance, and education; and they have required heavy taxation, levied in accordance with ability to pay. Meticulous regulation is another form, and housing, transportation, manufacturing, and commerce are fields subjected now to innumerable rules and orders. Or again it may appear as a paternalistic attempt to bolster weak members of the economic system through subsidies. Agriculture and shipping are recent beneficiaries. Whatever the methods employed, the social and economic fabric of England is being redesigned —to some at a rate perilously rapid, to others criminally slow. Whether fast or slow, the mature citizens of the nation have been living in a social revolution, and the England of their youth will not be the England of their old age.

Undoubtedly the World War accelerated the speed of this intervention by the state. Rights and interests were trampled upon rather indiscriminately by the nation in arms, and occasional protests were drowned in the huzzas of patriotic fervor. Powers once granted to governments are seldom handed back intact, and that has been the experience in postwar Britain. The tide has never ebbed to its original mark. D.O.R.A. remains to remind Englishmen that control through the central government hovers over all aspects of their lives.

Parliament, nominally the policy-forming arm of the state, in an effort to satisfy or attract millions of constituents, has written the statutes of the new order. It has retained its structure and the forms of past centuries, for this appeals to the British temperament; but lower chamber supremacy, more committees, closure, and other legislative devices give evidence of its attempts to keep pace with the tempo of the age. In the executive, new names indicate something of the change in the scope of state activity—Ministers of Health, Labor, Mines, and Transport—while investigation of the duties of the older officers would reveal startling changes from a century ago.

The increasing burden placed upon the governmental structure has revealed many inadequacies, and critics whose number is legion have, on paper, repaired and reconstructed it along more logical lines. The critics have taken Parliament to the surgery many times, and undoubtedly some major operations would have been performed long since if the doctors could have agreed upon their exact character. While few people would defend the House of Commons as an ideal legislative chamber, the political doctors would probably make only a few superficial operations upon it, but the House of Lords would be something entirely different when it came out from under the anesthetic. It has few apologists for its present structure, which defies virtually every canon of what a legislative chamber in a democratic state should be like. It represents a small aristocracy, it is overwhelmingly drawn from one political party, its membership is hereditary, and the duties of membership compete poorly with the business, social, and recreational interests of a majority of its peers. Its anachronistic character had been recognized long before the Parliament Act of 1911 reduced it to a distinctly secondary position. For almost a century the House had been sleeping in mediaeval splendor. There is a story that Mr. Labouchere, the nephew and not the son of Lord Taunton, was on one occasion met by an acquaintance who had confused this relationship. "Mr. Labouchere, I have just heard your father make an admirable speech in the House of Lords," this person said.

"Really?" said Labouchere. "My father has been dead some years, and I have always wondered where he had gone to."

And yet the House of Lords performs its critical and

revisory duties as a second chamber sufficiently well so that neither the reforming schemes of its friends nor those of its enemies arouse much enthusiasm. The Conservatives, apprehensive of a day of Labor ascendancy, would like to restore its veto power while retaining the dominance of the House of Commons, but since they have not discovered a formula for eating one's cake and having it too, the Lords remain unreformed. The Labor party would amputate the House entirely, but it has never had a free hand with the patient.

The Cabinet has also been the subject of much censorious examination. In the eighteenth century the Cabinet numbered from seven to nine. In the next century it grew to the seventeen of Lord Salisbury's second government, and by the time of the World War it usually contained about twenty members. A Cabinet of this size was generally regarded as too large for effective work, but still ministers representing new activities of the state seemed to merit membership in its highest council. "If only a few of them took part," said Lord Lansdowne in explaining this dilemma, "the cabinet ceased to be representative. If many of them took part, the proceedings tended to become prolix and interminable, and it is a matter of common knowledge that reasons of that kind led to the practice of transacting a good deal of the more important work of the government through the agency of an informal inner cabinet." [2] This inner council became a recognized group when Mr. Lloyd George, declaring that the War could not be won "by a Sanhedrin," created the War Cabinet of five (later six) members in December, 1916. After the War, hostility to the junto doomed the small Cabinet, and by 1923 the body was back to its prewar size. This restoration was against the advice of the Machinery of Government Committee, reporting to the Ministry of Reconstruction in 1918, which proposed a Cabinet of "preferably ten, or, at most,

[2] *House of Lords Official Report,* June 20, 1918.

twelve." [3] The debate on the proper size of the Cabinet still goes on, but except in the face of some national crisis demanding the exercise of dictatorial powers by a compact group the number is not likely to drop below twenty. Great impatience toward legislatures and their rather tedious methods of arriving at decisions is prevalent in the modern world, and in many countries the men of talk have been given a permanent vacation while the men of action try their hands. Even in England, the home of Parliamentary institutions, one major party has declared that their "forms were devised to suit the purposes of the negative state in the nineteenth century, and are definitely unsuited to the needs of the positive state in the twentieth." [4] Whether one agrees or not with the proposition that the traditional forms of Parliamentary government are ill-adapted to the new social and economic order, he may ask if the administrative system developed several generations ago suits an environment admittedly changed.

The British, faced with the increasing burden placed on government, have allowed their administrative staffs to expand without devising any radically different machinery for the new duties. The numbers give an indication of this expansion. Thus, in 1914, the Civil Service numbered 337,431; in 1934, it numbered 444,400. A few new departments have been added as the need for them has arisen, but the general structure has changed only slightly. When new functions have been assumed, they have generally been added to the most appropriate departments. Thus, with the nationalization of the telephone and the telegraph these services were given to the Post Office.

While, in general, no radical changes in administrative structure or practice have been introduced, two or three developments deserve mention. One important innovation

---

[3] Cmd. 9230 (1918), p. 5. This document is commonly known as the Haldane Report.
[4] "For Socialism and Peace," pamphlet containing Labor party's statement of policy, July, 1934, p. 27.

has occurred in recent years, and that is the creation of several public corporations to care for services which are state-owned but not directly subject to governmental policy. The British Broadcasting Corporation, the London Passenger Transport Board, and the Electricity Commissioners are outstanding examples. The B.B.C., which has a monopoly of radio broadcasting in Great Britain, is operated by a board of directors who select a director-general as the manager of the system, and the whole enterprise is nominally subject to the Postmaster-General, who is the Parliamentary representative of the corporation. This method insures public ownership, but not partisan direction of the service.

Increased Treasury control is a further administrative development of note. By Orders in Council in 1910 and 1920, Treasury control over the administrative staffs was greatly strengthened and departmental autonomy proportionately diminished.

The establishment of a Cabinet secretariat is another significant development. Under the stress of war conditions, the Cabinet created a secretariat which proved so useful that it has become a permanent part of the national administrative machinery. Its growth to the size of a small government department during the premiership of Mr. Lloyd George aroused criticism, and in 1922 the Bonar Law ministry deflated it considerably. The Cabinet secretariat remains, though, a vital part of the administrative system. Its able director for twenty years, Sir Maurice Hankey, is secretary of the important Committee of Imperial Defense and also clerk of the Privy Council. Upon him depends much of the responsibility for co-ordinating policies and practices of the ministerial departments.

There are demands from time to time that the whole administrative machine be recast. Critics say that it is poorly organized for its modern work: departmental duties overlap, co-ordination in the same field is lacking, and a complete reallocation of functions is necessary. The existence of three military departments is pointed to as the supreme folly of present-day administrative organization, and the suggested remedy is a single defense department which can co-ordinate the armed services.[5] The Haldane Report of 1918 presents the most impressive case for a general reorganization and regrouping of the central government's services.

If the administrative services were being created *de novo* there would probably be a somewhat different system of departments and functions, but it is not likely that there will ever be an opportunity for a thoroughly rational organization to be made, for in England they remodel but seldom clear the ground and build anew. So while it may be valuable to speculate on the perfect administrative system, such thoughts have little bearing on practical problems. When necessity requires a different system the British have a way of creating a practical arrangement that meets the situation. Thus the Committee of Imperial Defense satisfies the most plausible reason for a common defense department—co-ordination of military plans and forces—and it is questionable if unification of departments would produce any substantial economies. Again, the recent rearmament program has required the Prime Minister to appoint a deputy, with Cabinet rank, to assist him as chairman of the Committee. Entitled Minister for the Co-ordination of Defense, Sir Thomas W. H. Inskip, serves as chairman of important subcommittees and supervises the day-to-day work of the Committee of Imperial Defense.[6] Interdepartmental committees are a com-

---

[5] The Geddes Committee on National Expenditure recommended the creation of a single Ministry of Defense in 1922.—Cmd. 1581 (1922), pp. 8-9. However, the May Committee reported, "Our conclusion after careful review of all the evidence is that no substantial reduction of cost would follow from the creation of a Ministry of National Defense, and on the contrary there would be a serious risk that the efficiency of the Services might be impaired by the alteration of system involved."—Cmd. 3920 (1931), p. 64.

[6] See W. Ivor Jennings, *Cabinet Government* (New York, Macmillan, 1936), pp. 228-46, for an account of the evolution of the Committee of

mon feature of the administrative system, and they are set up when a question of policy or a problem of administration overlaps the boundaries of one department. The rearmament program supplies an illustration of this practice. The Treasury Interservice Committee is to be composed of representatives of the three fighting services under the chairmanship of a Treasury official. The Committee "will have power to authorize large contracts for munitions for any defense department prior to formal Treasury approval and otherwise to expedite transactions incidental to war preparations." [7]

The Economic Advisory Council has attempted to produce similar co-operation in respect to governmental policy on economic questions. Composed of the Prime Minister, the Chancellor of the Exchequer, the Secretary of State for the Dominions, the President of the Board of Trade, and the Minister of Agriculture and Fisheries, the Council uses experts from both within and without the departments. It has conducted a considerable amount of research into economic and scientific problems, but there is little evidence to indicate that its influence has extended much beyond the development of technical departmental policy.[8] "It has not been a success," one authority has said, "because neither the problems it was to study nor the resources of investigation which it might use were defined." [9]

One may expect an extension of the plan of creating autonomous corporations to handle certain public enterprises, for it is obvious that the management of business undertakings, such as operating buses and trams, requires a different organization than the execution of policy in colonial affairs or the supervision of national health. In

Imperial Defense and its present elaborate organization of committees and subcommittees.
[7] *The New York Times,* March 8, 1936.
[8] Jennings, *op. cit.,* pp. 247-49.
[9] K. B. Smellie, *A Hundred Years of English Government* (New York, Macmillan, 1937), p. 402.

addition to these bodies there are appearing outside the walls of the regular departments many official and quasi-official organizations which administer special services of one kind or another. They range from purely public bodies to private institutions performing certain governmental functions. "The dividing line between official organs and unofficial institutions," Professor W. A. Robson has said, "is becoming less and less distinct.... The increasing intervention of Government in economic affairs makes it probable that, whether we move in the direction of socialism or towards state-supported capitalism, a large increase will occur in the number of these miscellaneous bodies set up for particular purposes and manned chiefly by persons with experience in the industry or occupation concerned." [10]

The development of the state in new rôles as owner, partner, manager, regulator, and umpire of the complex activities of twentieth-century life has caused its forms to be subjected to searching examination and criticism. It is not the purpose of this study to pursue that investigation further, but rather to examine the type of personnel attracted to the organs of British government, particularly the executive and administrative arms, and their relationship to each other. Long ago Pope wrote,

> For forms of government let fools contest:
> Whate'er is best administered is best.

There remains a considerable element of truth in this dictum. Able men can do much to ameliorate the deficiencies of inadequate governmental machinery, and poor men can ruin the most perfect schemes.

England has had at times both able and poor personnel in her political offices. The spoils system once ruled as unblushingly in London as in the Washington of King Andrew. Long after the Great Reform Act of 1832 had

[10] "The Public Service," *The British Civil Servant* (London, 1937), pp. 25-26.

accomplished much in the reform of the House of Commons, the administrative services and the armed forces were still provinces of the spoilsman. But reform attacked these forts of inefficiency and corruption, and they eventually yielded. England was very fortunate in having as she entered the period of rapid social and economic change a national Civil Service of great efficiency and integrity, for without it much of the state's expansion into new areas of activity would have been done in a clumsy, blundering manner.

Three or four generations ago public life in Great Britain was the exclusive preserve of the upper classes. Their representatives sat in Parliament, held the seals of ministerial office, pronounced the law from the bench, and administered the law from government offices. But the march of political democracy in the nineteenth century made people in the lower strata of society technically eligible for public office; and as the new electorate, possessed of political equality, demanded a measure of security in the baffling industrial world in which it toiled, it sent its representatives into government to obtain its desires. The election of 1906 saw the influx of a considerable number of these representatives into Parliament—men who corresponded to no previous types.

This election of 1906 is a significant event in connection with the personnel of British political institutions. At the time it was almost as exciting a contest as the Derby for the London crowds which thronged the Embankment, Trafalgar Square, and Aldwych. During several January evenings magic lanterns threw faces and numbers on giant screens to announce election results, and the fringes of the huge crowds were informed by flashing red and blue lights. Rockets and colored fires, carrying news to waiting suburbanites, cast eerie hues over the masses, now cheering, now hooting as the results came in.

None standing in those streets had ever witnessed such

a general election. An expected Liberal victory was soon apparent, but the magnitude of the landslide was startling. Mr. Balfour lost his seat in East Manchester, and a dozen other Unionist occupants of the Treasury Bench went down to defeat. Not only were many of the Liberal victories surprising, but the Labor strength was a revelation. Holding old seats by large majorities, the Laborites routed Conservatives in numerous industrial areas. When the last returns were counted the Liberals had 397 seats, Labor had won 51, and the Irish Nationalists 83. The Unionist opposition numbered only 157.

As the campaign cries of "Tariff Reform," "Work for All," and "No Slavery" (a reference to the importation of indentured coolies in the Rand) subsided, there were some who perceived that this election was not just another phase of the contest between the "ins" and the "outs." Probably the crowds in the streets sensed a more than ordinary change. When the new House of Commons assembled the revolution was more apparent.

It was largely a House of youngish men, still more a House of "new" men in politics. Just as the Reform Bill of 1832 had added the manufacturer and the man of business to the aristocrat and the man of affairs, so the election of 1906 added to those classes in the House the man of ideas and the sociologist. For the first time the Commons contained a large number of men who had entered it, not on the strength of their hereditary position, their local importance, their forensic skill, or their intellectual reputation; but solely on the basis of their sociological enthusiasm and their political idealism. Never had there been a House so full of men whom a member in the late eighteenth century would have found it impossible to place in any category known to him. The type was, of course, more common on the Liberal side than among the Unionists; but even in the Opposition ranks could be found the man who had gone from his university, or even his school, into some activity of social reform, or some propaganda of the new political economy, and passed thence into Parliament. It is largely to that new political economy that we must look for the explanation of the general election of 1906.[11]

It is not only to Parliament that these "new" men have taken. Coming up through the elementary and secondary schools to the universities, they have sought entrance into all kinds of public life. They compete for posts in the Civil Service, sit on the councils of scores of local governments, and enter the administrative services of counties and boroughs. Since the World War their appearance has been in sufficient numbers to reveal to the old governing class that its day of hegemony was passing. Probably the creation of the first Labor government in 1924 brought the members of the traditional order face to face with the situation.

Certain questions arise in the minds of persons who have watched this revolution. One is whether the best traditions of the governing classes of yesterday will find root among the new people coming into power. For the governing classes have created certain traditions which have raised British government to a recognized high standard. The knightly code of *noblesse oblige,* translated into modern terms, has prompted the most capable members of the governing classes to make sacrifices and give devoted and loyal service to the state. Of course, it was often in the interest of their class to do so, for the state furnished them with positions of honor and profit; but still their code urged them on after their immediate desires had been satisfied to give their talent for the nation's welfare. Many simply fed upon the store of wealth accumulated by past generations, but the majority, to whom this parasitical life was open, too, chose to be of service as the standards of their day dictated.

It is to their credit that they greatly improved political morality in Britain. Their grandfathers left them a Par-

[11] R. H. Gretton, *A Modern History of the English People, 1880-1922* (New York, Dial Press, 1930), pp. 695-96.

liament of rotten boroughs and bribed and debauched electors; a civil service founded upon nepotism and spoils; a judicial system whose inhumanity was obscuring its essential virtue; and military services made incompetent by purchase and barbarity. They scrubbed out these Augean stables pretty thoroughly. It took them about a century to complete the job, and they naturally left a few piles of rubbish here and there, but by and large they infused most governmental institutions with a code of ethics that made them models to be emulated in other countries.

There is no feeling that this progress will be consciously abandoned, but rather a fear that the newly empowered classes will not appreciate the need for eternal vigilance. The fact that one is a son of the masses is no vaccination against all the ills to which political life is susceptible. A Croker or a Tweed could probably have taught a Walpole or a Newcastle a few new wrinkles in the electoral arts.

Another question is whether the best talent of all classes, now that all are partners in the business, will be drawn to politics. There has been some fear that the supposedly disillusioned youth of the postwar years would shun politics as something invented by a discredited generation which preceded him. The scales are favorably weighted in this case, for as an Englishman has said with much truth: "Political life has been for centuries the focus and centre of English activities. And in a way that distinguishes us from other peoples. For though there is a sense in which the 'political' life is the centre of every nation's activities —is, in fact, the sum-total of them—there is a special sense in which for us politics have been a common ground upon which all kinds of activities meet, a field of action at once more comprehensive, universal and representative than any other." [12] It is this universal interest which will probably draw capable people of all classes into the political

[12] A. L. Rowse, *Politics and the Younger Generation* (London, 1931), p 11.

orbit. There have been built up in England certain inducements to a political life which, added to the tradition of *noblesse oblige,* were powerful influences attracting talent from the old governing classes. They may not be so strong now that their exclusive character has largely been destroyed—in fact, there is a good deal of evidence that they are not—but still there remains the lure of political life to a people bred to it, to be reinforced by what habit and tradition remain. To the youth from the lower social classes political life will undoubtedly be as attractive as a pretty garden, which their fathers could view only through the gates, but to which education and democracy have given this generation the keys.

A further question is whether the governing classes and the new classes in politics can work together harmoniously —without suspicion and mistrust. Until recently it usually was not difficult for politicians, civil servants, judges, or other public officers to co-operate, for they sprang from the same social stratum. They came from the same schools and universities and they met socially at country houses and clubs. In fact, in all their contacts certain assumptions were always present and never open to debate. Political life today is bringing together people from quite diverse backgrounds. Can they and will they tolerate and respect each other's views, or must they dissipate their strength in internal struggles for power? Will they preserve their sense of fair play, for which their nation has been distinguished, and permit British institutions to evolve along lines advantageous to the country as a whole?

No conclusive answers can yet be given to the questions discussed. This is a period in some ways of tradition-breaking, and it is too early to say which ones will come through intact and which will be relegated to histories of past manners and customs. England will be fortunate if these questions are answered in such a manner that she will have political institutions energized and reinvigorated by the best talent thrown up by the whole nation, and public officers carrying on the noblest traditions of what was once a governing class.

It is the purpose of this study to present some of the social and educational backgrounds of two important classes of public officers in Great Britain—members of Parliament and civil servants; to indicate the inducements to public life which influence these people; and to analyze their relationships as the personnel of important branches of the government.

When an American is challenged with a British comparison unfavorable to some aspect of his political institutions, his reaction is frequently, "Well, they get a better class of people in public life in England." There are signs that the American is becoming hopeful of improving the personnel of his political institutions;[13] and if it be true that his British cousins have preceded him in this regard, perhaps an indication of how capable people are attracted to English public life will be helpful in his task. The British are facing the problem of adjusting their traditional institutions to new democratic conditions and, while this does not correspond to anything in the American scene, its performance is interesting from the standpoint of the development of political and social structures.

As a background to the contemporary situation in Great Britain the state of public affairs about a century ago is important, for much of what is admired in British government is the product only of nineteenth-century reform. The following chapter attempts a survey of the character and development of the national public services during this reforming period.

[13] Reports, for example, of the Commission of Inquiry on Governmental Personnel and the President's Committee on Administrative Management.

CHAPTER II

The Old Officialdom and Its Reform

Parliament

ENGLISH history of the eighteenth and early nineteenth centuries is studded with the great deeds of heroic, brilliant men. The military successes of Marlborough, Clive, Wolfe, Nelson, and Wellington will always shine brightly in the annals of Britain; the statesmanship of Chatham and his son ranks them as men of genius; the oratory of Burke and Fox, challenging Englishmen to preserve their liberal heritage, is a permanent treasure of the nation. Yet all these are brilliant flashes against a rather sordid background of public life. We have Wellington's word that his Peninsular soldiers were the scum of the earth, and Nelson sailed in vessels filled by the press gang. The eloquence of great statesmen was addressed to politicians so professional that one prime minister kept a tariff listing every man's price. Public offices staffed with the impecunious relatives of public figures and the beneficiaries of powerful patrons were the rule of the day. It was a period when money talked with far more effectiveness than today. Scarcely anything was safe from being knocked down to the highest bidder. Lord Chesterfield's offer of £2,500 for a seat in the House of Commons for his son was laughingly spurned by the brokers; nabobs from the East had with gross indecency run up the price to £5,000. Bolingbroke's candid statement of the attitude of the Tories of his day toward public office would do for either party for a century after his time. "I am afraid," he said, "that we came to court in the same disposition as all parties have done;

that the principal spring of our actions was to have the government of the State in our hands; that our principal views were the conservation of this power, great employments to ourselves, and great opportunities of rewarding those who had helped to raise us, and of hurting those who had stood in opposition to us." [1]

From this base state of political morality much progress has been made. There have been great improvements in the ways of selecting all types of public officials, and with them has come a considerable change for the better in the general quality of public servants. Merit, which formerly had to bow to claims of position, influence, and wealth, is now the usual criterion to success in official life. This is not to suggest that in modern Britain nepotism, patronage, and the influence of wealth are definitely banished, but it may be said that they are no longer the prevailing forces in public life, and when they appear the parties concerned are on the defensive to explain their actions to a watchful opposition and a critical electorate. No government today could take pride in defending the Empire with forces composed of the riffraff of the world and commanded by incompetents who had purchased their places of honor and trust; no politician could openly find places on the public payroll for his dependents and people to whom he was personally indebted; and no constituency could be debauched with ale and pound notes at election time. With demagoguery and hypocrisy present-day politics has evils aplenty, but the public conscience has progressed to the point where the grosser forms of corruption must be rigidly eschewed or performed always with the risk of discovery and consequent punishment. Those who desire to serve the public today at its expense must at least make a convincing pretense of merit and proficiency.

The story of the reform of the House of Commons has been told many times. Even when Blackstone was offering

---

[1] Quoted in Esmè Wingfield-Stratford, *The History of British Civilization* (New York, 1928), II, 642.

his panegyric on the English constitution to the world an occasional voice of protest over the rotten borough system was heard. As a youthful member of the House, and a beneficiary of the patronage system, William Pitt advocated a reform in the methods of electing members. However, he was only briefly a leader of Parliamentary reform, for the burden of ministerial office and the cares of state diverted his interest. Any impetus the reforming movement might have gained in the late eighteenth century was checked by English revulsion at the course of the French Revolution; and after the titanic struggle with Napoleon Bonaparte the inevitable Eldonish reaction set in. Anything hinting of liberalism could create a panic such as afflicted the magistrates at Peterloo. The spectre of the guillotine fell over England just as Red firing squads became nightmares to the Western nations after the World War.

Had the social and economic life of England remained static during this period reform might have been postponed a long time, but, as everyone knows, the steam engine and the accompanying mechanical inventions were creating another new England—this time within the mother country itself. From this new England rose a demand for social reforms and the right to participate in the political system, and it could not be ignored. The result was the Reform Act of 1832.

As a revolutionary measure the Reform Act of 1832 was cast in a very modest mold. Fifty-six pocket boroughs which had usually been the virtual property of aristocratic patrons, thirty seats from small towns, and two from the City of London were distributed among the new centers of population in the north. The county franchise of 40s. freeholders was extended to £10 copyholders and leaseholders and £50 tenants-at-will, and the borough vote to £10 rate-payers. Altogether almost half a million voters were added to the rolls.

While the Act of 1832 effected no change in the qualifications for membership in Parliament it did through a broadening of the electorate introduce a new kind of political figure. "I never saw so many shocking bad hats in my life," exclaimed the Duke of Wellington after his first sight of the reformed Parliament. The principal people enfranchised were the upper middle class of the cities, and they naturally elected representatives of their industrial and commercial interests. The ruling classes of the past were still dominant, and as the new possessors of political power usually desired to emulate the landed aristocracy there was no sharp cleavage with former generations. However, the man whose name and fame rested on business was an increasingly familiar figure at Westminster.

The Reform Act of 1832 was the beginning of a series of measures which during the past century has broadened the electorate to include more than half the population of Great Britain. In 1867 approximately a million voters were added by lowering the property qualifications in the counties for copyholders, leaseholders, and tenants-at-will and enfranchising £10 lodgers in the boroughs. The urban working classes were the chief beneficiaries of this Tory legislation. The Liberals extended similar privileges to the counties in 1884 which meant an addition of about two million voters, chiefly among the miners and rural working classes. The next year the Redistribution Act made representation in the House of Commons considerably more equitable from a geographical point of view. For a number of years before the World War the suffrage issue was a live one in English politics, and both Liberals and Conservatives attempted to pass measures widening the electorate still further and distributing the seats more evenly. But the inability to get substantial agreement among the many interests involved postponed all legislation until war conditions made some radical change necessary. In 1916 a commission, the Speaker's Conference, representing all parties and the advocates of different reform movements, drafted a far-reaching measure which reached the statute books in 1918 as the Representation of the People Act. Sweeping away the old property qualifications and the distinction between borough and county suffrage, it put representation upon the basis of citizenship and added more than twelve million people to the voting rolls. About eight and one-half million of these new voters were women, and in 1928 the remaining women who were outside the pale were admitted on the same basis as men. Today approximately 27,000,000 men and women are eligible to vote in general elections—the culmination of a century's reform of the suffrage.

Each suffrage measure has to some degree broadened the composition of the House of Commons itself. While the newly enfranchised groups have not by any means turned exclusively to their own ranks for their representatives, there has been a disposition for the laboring classes to elect fellow workmen and trade union officials to Parliament, just as the manufacturer and the man of business were to be found in politics after the Act of 1832. This has proceeded so far that the Labor party has displaced the Liberal party as one of the two principal political groups of the country.

The process of removing a number of qualifications for membership in the House of Commons accompanied the expansion of the electorate. From severe limitations upon membership in the best club in London the legal bars have been let down until almost any British citizen who can get himself elected is eligible. The East Indian Communist Saklatvala has sat with the bluest blood of Albion. Religious tests, except that barring clergymen of the Churches of England and Scotland and the Roman Catholic Church, disappeared. The property qualification was removed in 1858. Previously every county member had to possess a minimum income from land of £600 annually and a borough member, £300. The Tories had introduced this rule in 1711 to bar from the House any Whigs who were rich but soiled by trade, and Dean Swift said that this measure was "the greatest security that was ever contrived for preserving the Constitution, which otherwise might in a little time be wholly at the mercy of the monied interest." Impecunious candidates with the proper connections habitually evaded it by having property temporarily deeded to them. Once in, they surrendered the deeds. To one Edward Auchmuty Glover seems to go the honor of causing the repeal of the property qualification, although the Chartists had agitated against it in their heyday. Glover, elected to Parliament in 1857 for the Yorkshire borough of Beverley, was suspected of being a sort of intruder in sacred precincts as yet unaccustomed to wild men from the Clyde and similar present-day phenomena. He was unseated for not possessing the necessary property, prosecuted for perjury, and sentenced to Newgate. Then the House, evidently ashamed of its hypocrisy since many of its members had connived at the practice of fictitious conveyances which had admitted such men as Burke, Pitt, and Fox, repealed the Act of 1711.

The elimination of corruption in elections has done a great deal to raise the moral tone of English politics and to give the candidate of modest means an opportunity to win a seat. Despite laws against bribery and other corrupt practices, eighteenth-century elections were conducted with the most shameless buying and selling of votes. In many constituencies seats habitually went to the candidates spending the most to win the voters' favor. One righteously inclined candidate in an Irish constituency is said to have appealed to the parish priest to condemn in a sermon the acceptance of bribes. The priest preached a strong sermon, even threatening those who sold their votes with the prospect of going to hell. "Next day the candidate met one of the electors and asked what was the effect of Sunday's sermon. 'Your honor,' said he, 'votes have risen. We always got £20 for a vote before we knew it was a sin to sell it; but as his reverence tells us that we will be damned for selling our votes, we can't for the future afford to take less than £40.' " [2]

Electoral corruption was not proceeded against seriously until the latter half of the nineteenth century. A statute in 1854, provisions of the Ballot Act of 1872, and the Corrupt and Illegal Practices Prevention Act of 1883 virtually eliminated this black spot in English political life. The Act of 1883 not only prohibited corrupt practices but also outlawed such practices as hiring conveyances on election day and paying the expenses of voters to return to cast their ballots. Viscount Ullswater related that as a candidate in Rutland in the last election before this statute he had a very diligent agent who "began operations by chartering every available conveyance for taking electors to the poll and by communicating with all out-voters and sending them return tickets to Oakham. One gentleman eventually came all the way from the south of France to vote—at my expense." [3] By prohibitions of such practices and limits to the amounts candidates might spend in their campaigns, the scales were not so unfairly weighted in favor of wealthy politicians. A great deal is still spent in "nursing" constituencies, and the actual campaigns are not cheap adventures, but buying one's way into the House of Commons is not the certain route to Westminster that it once was.

The latter half of the nineteenth century also saw the military services changed from the bands of ruffians and Irish seeking escape from starvation, kept in order by torture and barbarous discipline, to fairly respectable short service organizations. The officer class was considerably improved by the abolition of the purchase of commissions, a practice which had allowed any incompetent with a few thousand pounds to obtain the command of troops. The horrors of the Crimean War, a struggle into which Eng-

---

[2] M. MacDonagh, *The Pageant of Parliament*, I, 27.
[3] Rt. Hon. James William Lowther, Viscount Ullswater, *A Speaker's Commentaries* (London, 1925), I, 154.

OLD OFFICIALDOM AND ITS REFORM

land got for no good reason that anyone could think of, aroused a sentiment which led to the substitution of merit for purchase.

Democratization of the military services has proceeded slowly. The Army especially has remained one of the most exclusive institutions in England. Consequently, Englishmen gasped in December, 1937, when the Secretary of State for War, Mr. Leslie Hore-Belisha, suddenly announced the retirement of fifty ranking "brass hats" and the appointment of the comparatively young Viscount Gort as head of the Army Council. Conservative governments can sometimes deal with vested rights in a way which would be considered sacrilegious if done by others.

The Civil Service: The Beginning of Reform

The Crimean War was also partly responsible for another reform movement which eventually transformed the Civil Service from a very indifferent corps of officials into an administrative organization without a peer in the world. The incompetence of governmental departments revealed by the strain of war caused the public to support a reform of the Civil Service which a number of politicians had already seen was long overdue.[4]

The steps toward this change date from the decade of the fifties of the last century. Prior to this time public offices were dispensed by the political party which happened to be in power. During the eighteenth century the King's right to make personal appointments had been hedged about and had deteriorated with the growth of the constitutional monarchy. With the removal of the government departments from the civil list and their maintenance by special Parliamentary grants the monarch had

---

[4] As Mr. K. B. Smellie has aptly said, "The Crimean War suggested that if Britons had never yet been slaves, their freedom was due more to geography and luck than to the efficiency of the War Office."—*Op. cit.*, p. 108.

gradually receded from his position of personal influence over actual administration of the realm, and in place of seeking royal favor the aspirant to a public office cultivated the attention of a member of Parliament, who, if he had no place available himself, might speak to a minister or the patronage secretary of the Treasury.

Sporadic attempts were made to clean from the departmental payrolls many obsolete offices which carried fat salaries but required little or no work from their occupants. The abolition of these sinecures was stoutly resisted by their holders and their friends, but gradually the majority of them yielded to earnest demands for economy and efficiency. The logic employed by one old barnacle of the time is typical of the defense made for these plums of the patronage system. This holder of a sinecure paying £3,000 a year was threatened with the reduction of his salary to a very modest stipend, and he protested vigorously on the ground that no cut in remuneration could be made without a proportionate reduction in duties. Since he had no duties to be reduced, it was logically impossible to reduce his salary, he argued. Naturally, short work was made of such arguments unless the occupant of the place had connections at court or in high office.

Many accounts from contemporary literature picture the effects of the patronage system. None is better than Anthony Trollope's *The Three Clerks*. The author wrote with some authority as he had served in the Post Office for many years. But it is not necessary to seek in fiction for evidence concerning the incompetence and inefficiency existing in many of the departments. Damaging statements came from the lips of civil servants themselves. In 1854 R. M. Bromley, Accountant-General of the Navy, wrote: "The most feeble sons in families which have been so fortunate as to obtain an appointment, yes, and others too, either mentally or physically incapacitated, enter the Service.... The more able and ambitious sons seek the open professions.... I have known many instances of individuals baldly stating they were not put into the Service by their patrons to work." [5]

Sir James Stephen, Under Secretary of State for the Colonies, testified after spending thirty-five years in the public service that "the majority of the members of the Colonial Department in my time, possessed only a low degree, and some of them in a degree almost incredibly low, either the talents or the habits of men of business, or the industry, the zeal or the knowledge required for the effective performance of their appropriate functions." [6]

Popular belief in the lax discipline in the public departments led Edwin Chadwick to state that "previous service in Government offices has, in reality, operated as a powerful objection to candidates for employment in commercial houses." [7]

However, it should not be presumed that the old Civil Service was rotten throughout and that Whitehall was a row of asylums for deficient but harmless dependents of the governing classes. The mere fact that the public business was carried on is proof that some capable men sat at government desks. England was the most powerful country in the world at the time, and a service of fools carrying on the general business of government could not have aided Britain in attaining her position or held it once secured. Also the names of some civil servants of the first half of the ninteenth century indicate that the service included a fair sprinkling of competent officials. Sir James Stephen, Major Graham, Rowland Hill, Edward Romilly, Herman Merivale, Sir Thomas Francis Fremantle, Dr. Lyon Playfair, Stafford Northcote, John Stuart Mill, and Sir Charles E. Trevelyan were all permanent civil servants about the middle of the century, and most of them made the service their career. Sir James Stephen was probably

[5] "Papers Relating to the Reorganization of the Civil Service," *Parliamentary Papers* (1854-55), XX, 53.
[6] *Ibid.*, p. 73.
[7] *Ibid.*, p. 138.

correct when he said the service was "clearly distinguishable into three classes." The first class possessed "qualities of which I can still never think without the highest admiration and respect—such as a large capacity of mind, literary powers of rare excellence, sound scholarship, indomitable energy, mature experience in public affairs, and an absolute devotion to the Public Service. It comprised some men who must have risen to eminence in any field of open competition, and who, if born to more ample fortunes, might reasonably have aspired to hold the seals of office in which they were serving as subordinates." [8] The second class was composed of men who "performed diligently, faithfully, and judiciously the duties to which they were called; and those duties were, not rarely, such as belonged to ministers of state, than to the clerks in the office of such a minister." [9] Practically all of them were indebted to some patron for their appointment. The last class, which Sir James regretted to say outnumbered the other two, consisted of very incompetent clerks "appointed to gratify the political, the domestic, or the personal feelings of their patrons." [10]

If England suffered from the patronage system she was spared its vicious corollary, rotation of office. An exchange of power between Whigs and Tories did not mean the filling of virtually the whole Civil Service with adherents of the victorious party as practiced in the United States at the time—and not totally abandoned even today. Once appointed to a government position a young man was assured of a permanent place and a reasonable salary until he cared to retire.

There are several reasons why the system of rotation in office did not appear in England. One is that Englishmen had never been exposed to all the philosophical outpourings against long-term offices, hereditary right, and the need of special fitness for public office. In America, Revolutionary theorists had stressed the necessity of keep-

[8] *Ibid.*, pp. 72-73.   [9] *Ibid.*, p. 73.   [10] *Ibid.*

ing government close to the people by frequent elections, short terms, and the admission of the right of any citizen to occupy any office. Britons were quite accustomed to permanent tenure, and their public life, from the King down to a host of minor dignitaries, was full of life-time positions. The English tradition of respect for vested interests also supported the custom of permanent tenure of office.[11] But probably the most important reason why there was no rotation is to be found in the governmental system. Since the ministry had no definite term of office and was subject to sudden dismissal, a permanent civil service was a necessity to prevent a chaotic condition in public business at every shift of party fortunes. Of course, cabinets in nineteenth-century England did not appear and disappear with the rapidity that has characterized some of the postwar imitators of English government, but there were periods when the practice of the policy of rotation in office would have brought the government's routine work to a standstill. And with so little certainty of tenure it would also have been difficult to recruit even a service of placemen.

So the patronage system extended no further than the right of the party in office to fill with its partisans the places which fell vacant in the natural course of events—through death, retirement, or resignation. Probably the appetites of the members of Parliament were tempered by the consideration that their patronage was not a particularly effective tool for securing re-election. It helped, of course, to get a place at the Admiralty for the son of a neighboring squire who wasn't just sure what was to become of his wayward Henry, but such patronage was less valuable than the right of naming a score of postmasters, whose fence-building activities are stimulated by the per-

---

[11] Cf. A. Lawrence Lowell, *The Government of England* (New York, 1909), I, 153-54. Former President Lowell believes that "the sentiment that a man has a vested interest in the office he holds" accounted for the absence of rotation in office in England.

fect realization that they and their patron rise and fall together. The corrupting influence of the patronage system on the members of Parliament was loudly denounced, but that side of the evil was rather exaggerated: there were scarcely enough offices available. The politicians were principally concerned in taking care of their dependents —poor relatives and family friends. The public injury arose from the incompetence of many of these appointees rather than from the degradation of the patrons.

Yet England's escape from a policy of rotation in office was not an unmitigated blessing, for the assurance of permanent tenure made an incompetent clerk even more worthless. If he was devoid of ambition—and naturally an incompetent clerk almost invariably was—he merely had to perform the minimum that his superiors demanded and he basked serenely in the assurance that he had a life sinecure.

Responsibility had to be concentrated in the hands of a few capable officials in the departments where a majority of the civil servants were of poor quality, and these overworked men often became little autocrats and high priests of routine procedure which exasperated their political superiors and the public with whom they dealt. In the fifties and sixties bureaucratic despotism par excellence governed the conduct of the Colonial Office where Herman Merivale and Frederic Rogers were the chief permanent officials. Rogers was Mr. Mothercountry incarnate.[12] Colonials had to deal with Mr. Mothercountry, and all transactions were reduced to immutable rules which his efficient mind had thoroughly mastered. Of course, the evils existing in this colonial administration were due in large part to the indifference of ministers to imperial affairs, but they were fostered by a civil service

[12] Cf. Lowell, *op. cit.*, I, 177-80. "George Higinbotham, an Australian politician, spoke in 1869 of the colonies as having 'been really governed during the whole of the last fifteen years by a person named Rogers.'" *Dictionary of National Biography*, XVII, 120.

system in which the competent clerks had to be strong-willed and worshippers of precedent in order to perform the matters entrusted to them.

It is obviously impossible to characterize the Civil Service prior to 1855 as either good, bad, or fair. Some departments, like the fictitious Weights and Measures of Trollope's satire, were well managed and on the whole staffed by competent clerks. To England's good fortune, the revenue departments belonged to this superior class. Others were replicas of his Internal Navigation Office. The officials were dull and lazy, and discipline had long since vanished. In between there were departments conducted by competent civil servants whose efforts were encumbered by the barnacles which the patronage system nourished. Several departments had raised the *esprit de corps* of their staffs by promoting for merit alone, but in others the rewards fell to political and personal favorites. The task of reform, therefore, was to raise the quality of the poorer departments to a standard already existing in a few divisions of the government.

The reforming zeal of the early thirties, pent up in England for many years by revulsion at the excesses of the French Revolution and by an admiration for the constitutional monarchy which eighteenth-century Britain had evolved, soon spent itself, and a reform of the Civil Service was not included before the fire burned low. By the end of the decade the Whigs were holding office more from habit than the knowledge of power, and Macaulay described the ministry as a patronage bureau "distributing the loaves and fishes." To Carlyle, Parliament was simply the place where "hungry Greek was throttling down hungry Greek on the floor of St. Stephen until the loser cried, 'Hold, the place is thine.'"

As deeply entrenched as the patronage system seemed to be, ministers were not unreceptive to some change. Caustic tirades like Carlyle's were indicating public disgust, but they had been heard before. Politicians might ignore them; but certain facts were making an impression. As the number of officials increased the distribution of patronage became a good deal of a burden. By 1851 the clerical service numbered 17,815, while the total number of civil employees was 53,578.[13] The number was growing rapidly, and in 1860 there were about 103,000 persons employed as civil servants of the Crown, although almost half of these were artisans, laborers, or temporary workers.[14] At the same time the legislative and administrative work of the ministers was demanding more time, and some of them were willing to be rid of the perpetual annoyance of place-seekers. With the enlargement of the electorate after 1832 patronage became less useful for the purpose of endearing an ordinary member of Parliament to his constituents, for he had no great number of places to distribute and English party organization had not developed to the point where tactful appointments could keep a machine well lubricated. Patronage assisted the ministry in keeping backbenchers in line, but still it was not the resource that it has been to the American President and dissolution was a satisfactory substitute. No small number of the members of Parliament resisted the loss of patronage after the government committed itself to reform. For a time they blocked a change, but in a few years the apologists of patronage melted away. The success of the Civil Service reformers indicates not so much an unusual moral sense in public life (although the Victorian *ton* was somewhat above that of her two royal predecessors), but an appreciation on the part of ministers that an efficient, nonpartisan administrative system would relieve them of the bothers of office-seekers and give them a reliable corps of subordinates. More and more the political officials were finding it necessary to leave important functions to the permanent staffs. If the ministers were to be held re-

[13] "Papers Relating to the Reorganization of the Civil Service," *Parliamentary Papers* (1854-55), XX, 439.

[14] Robert Moses, *The Civil Service of Great Britain* (New York, 1914), p. 108.

sponsible for the actions of their departments they had to be assured that the business was being conducted by fairly competent officials.

Official steps toward reform began in 1848. Sir Charles E. Trevelyan, one of the principal authors of Civil Service reform, admitted later that "the revolutionary period gave us a shake and created a disposition to put our house in order." [15] A Treasury minute dated November 3, 1848, authorized an inquiry into that department, since it was obviously the logical place to begin. The Treasury employed a large staff, and through its financial control exerted a considerable degree of superintendence over the other departments. Some of the chief officers of the Treasury were found to be overworked, and some of the divisions needed to be consolidated and reorganized in the interests of efficiency. The report also condemned the practice of public officials serving as directors of banking and commercial companies "by which they contract obligations inconsistent with their official position, and absent themselves periodically during the hours of business." Promotion by merit only was emphatically approved.

It is indispensable for the efficiency and character of the Office that those persons only should be promoted who feel an active interest in their duties, and take pains to qualify themselves for the higher employment of the Department.... The habits which make valuable public servants are generally formed in early life; and it is right that a young man should feel, from his first entering the Office, that his future advancement will depend upon his own conduct.[16]

The Treasury already appointed only after a qualifying examination and a year's probation. Of course this policy was approved. Practically all the recommendations were accepted by the Treasury Board in a minute dated March 27, 1849.

[15] *Parliamentary Papers* (1875), XXIII, 100.
[16] "Reports of Committees of Inquiry into Public Offices," *Parliamentary Papers* (1854), VII, 11.

The inquiry into the Treasury establishment was followed in the next four years by a series of investigations into practically all the government departments. Trevelyan was joined by Stafford Northcote, and under the aegis of Gladstone, the Chancellor of the Exchequer, they composed a team of expert inquisitors. Trevelyan after graduation from the famous Haileybury school for training Indian civil servants had had a notable career in India. Upon his return he was made Assistant Secretary in the Treasury. Northcote, educated at Eton and Balliol, Oxford, had won Gladstone's esteem as his private secretary. As Vice-President of the Board of Trade Northcote had gained practical experience in the Civil Service. A little later he transferred his abilities to politics and entered the House of Commons as a Conservative. The inquiries and reports of Trevelyan and Northcote were made most valuable by the fact that their combined knowledge and experience included familiarity with the educational system, occupancy of varied and important administrative posts, and the possession of a genuine zeal for the improvement of the public service.

The Trevelyan-Northcote investigations produced reports on the Colonial Office, the Board of Trade, the Poor Law Board, the Privy Council Office, the Copyhold, Enclosure and Tithe Commission, the Colonial Land and Emigration Office, the Board of Ordnance, the Office of Works, and the Post Office. The deficiencies of the Service were practically the same in all these departments. Most of them were poorly organized, and as a result the burden of work falling upon different officials varied enormously. Obsolete offices existed, such as the Mail Coach Office with its inspectors of mail coaches and mail guards in the Post Office. Not only were these necessary establishments of the Georgian era still existent, but the investigators found that some of the methods of bookkeeping had not been changed since the reign of Queen Anne. In the Colonial Office they found that "according to the *theory*

OLD OFFICIALDOM AND ITS REFORM 33

of the office, a clerk can reach the first class only after he has been promoted three times on the ground of superior merit;... but... the *habit* has been to promote everybody in his turn...." [17] In some offices the theory was not even recognized.

Trevelyan and Northcote had the same remedies to propose for all these departments. Offices should be consolidated and the staffs more equitably distributed according to the labor to be performed, improved business methods introduced, appointment after examination and a period of probation, and promotion by merit. To the credit of the department heads, they accepted many of the recommendations, which were then given effect by Treasury minutes. However, the Treasury Lords rejected the proposal to change the appointment of lower class postmasters. All those receiving less than £175 were still to be named by the Treasury "after consulting, through the recommendations of the members for the county or town, the convenience and wishes of the population." The patronage in postmasters has a curious faculty for resisting reform.

Trevelyan and Northcote concluded their investigations with a report (November 23, 1853) on the state of the entire administrative system, and it is this report and its recommendations that have been the foundation for the modern British Civil Service. They opened the report with a statement of the defects of the Service: the absence of competition among candidates for appointment, the sense of security given incompetent officials, appointment by patronage, and advancement by seniority. "Admission to the Civil Service is indeed eagerly sought after, but it is for the unambitious, and the indolent or incapable, that it is chiefly desired." [18] Their general proposition for the improvement of the Service was briefly stated:

---
[17] *Ibid.*, pp. 50-51.
[18] "Report on the Organization of the Permanent Civil Service," *Parliamentary Papers* (1854), XXVII, 4.

The general principle, then, which we advocate is, that the public service should be carried on by the admission into its lower ranks of a carefully selected body of young men, who should be employed from the first upon work suited to their capacities and their education, and should be made constantly to feel that their promotion and future prospects depend entirely upon the industry and ability with which they discharge their duties, that with average abilities and reasonable application they may look forward constantly to a certain provision for their lives, that with superior powers they may rationally hope to obtain to the highest prizes in the Service, while if they prove decidedly incompetent, or incurably indolent, they must expect to be removed from it.[19]

Their "carefully selected body of young men" was to be secured by regular, competitive examinations conducted by a central board of examiners. The examinations were to be in liberal and cultural studies, and while they might be conducted to secure men with particular qualifications they were not to be framed for special appointments. The higher ranks were to be recruited from men between nineteen and twenty-five years of age; the lower ranks, between seventeen and twenty-one.

The authors of the report believed an Act of Parliament was necessary to accomplish this far-reaching change.

The existing system is supported by long usage and powerful interests; and were any government to introduce material alterations into it, in consequence of their own convictions, without taking the precaution to give those alterations the force of law, it is almost certain that they would be imperceptibly, or perhaps avowedly, abandoned by their successors, if they were not even allowed to fall into disuse by the very government which had originated them.[20]

Appended to the report was a letter from the Reverend Benjamin Jowett, of Balliol College, Oxford, to Sir Charles Trevelyan. Jowett had two objections to the re-

[19] *Ibid.*, p. 9.   [20] *Ibid.*, p. 23.

OLD OFFICIALDOM AND ITS REFORM

port. First, no assurance was given of the candidates' moral character; and second, the proposed examinations would be too intricate and cover too broad a field. These were not unsurmountable objections, however, as he included remedies for them. Testimonials and references would satisfy the character requirement, and for the examinations Jowett proposed four "schools": (1) classical literature; (2) mathematics and practical science; (3) political economy, moral philosophy, and law; (4) modern languages, history, and international law. Candidates would be examined in two or three "schools," with certain ones required for different departments. Jowett's recommendations became a portion of the report.

Before noticing the reception accorded the report it is important to mention a parallel reform which profoundly influenced Trevelyan and Northcote. This was the introduction of open competition and examinations in liberal studies for the candidates of the Indian Civil Service. The champion of this change was Trevelyan's brother-in-law, Lord Macaulay.

The achievement of this goal in the administration of the great British subcontinent had had a long history. The fabulous wealth accumulated in the eighteenth century by the oftentimes unscrupulous servants of the East India Company is a familiar story. The nineteenth century saw the crew of adventurous plunderers transformed into an exceptionally high-class corps of administrative officials. William Pitt's India Bill of 1784, which corrected the anomaly of the Company's performing civil and military functions, did not disturb the patronage it dispensed, and considering the attitude of the politicians of the day toward patronage the omission was probably wise. However, a little later the Company itself undertook to improve its household. Lord Wellesley, whom Macaulay termed "the most eminent member of the aristocracy who ever governed India," had established a training school for Indian writers, i.e., civil servants, at Fort William, and in 1806 the directors of the Company founded a college at Haileybury for the training of all Indian officials before they proceeded to the East. While the Company controlled the appointments to Haileybury, its entrance examinations and the quality of its work were high enough to insure that few but competent men received positions. After the Company lost its trade monopoly in 1833 it became little more than a patronage bureau, and in 1837 Macaulay attempted to have open competition introduced. But the directors "were not going to resign, without a struggle, the most valuable patronage since the days when the Roman Senate sent proconsuls and propraetors to Syria, Sicily, and Egypt." [21]

When the Company's charter was again before Parliament in 1853, Macaulay was more successful. His plan for open competition was accepted, thanks to the aid of Robert Lowe at the Board of Control, and the Company's appointing privileges abolished. He vigorously defended examinations in liberal studies, rather than tests of specialized knowledge, as the best means for securing the young men desired.

We believe that men who have been engaged, up to one or two and twenty, in studies which have no immediate connection with the business of any profession, and of which the effect is merely to open, to invigorate, and to enrich the mind, will generally be found, in the business of every profession, superior to men who have, at eighteen or nineteen, devoted themselves to the special studies of their calling.[22]

The principles advocated by Macaulay were embodied in the Trevelyan-Northcote report on the home Civil Service. Parliament accepted them in the Indian case. Would it do so for the domestic government?

[21] Sir George O. Trevelyan, *Life and Letters of Lord Macaulay* (London, 1908), p. 113.
[22] Quoted in A. Lawrence Lowell, and H. M. Stephens, *Colonial Civil Service; the Selection and Training of Colonial Officers in England, Holland, and France* (New York, 1900), pp. 81-82.

The report received a mixed reception. Most of the principal civil servants were sympathetic with any improvements in the Service, but many strongly resented the implications made against the existing corps of officials. John Stuart Mill regarded the selection of civil servants by competitive examination "to be one of those great public improvements the adoption of which would form an era in history." But at the same time the plan was ridiculed in unofficial circles as Utopian, Prussian, Chinese, and republican. It was designed to take the government out of the hands of the aristocracy and admit persons untrained as gentlemen. On the other hand, it was charged that the new examinations would give an undue preference to the upper classes. *The Times* was one of the few periodicals supporting the report.

Queen Victoria, "although not without considerable misgivings, sanctions the proposed plan, trusting that Mr. Gladstone will do what he can, in the arrangements of the details of it, to guard against the dangers, which she has pointed out.... A check, for instance, would be necessary upon the admission of candidates to compete for employment, securing that they should be otherwise eligible, besides the display of knowledge which they exhibit under examination." [23] Mr. Gladstone took pains to reassure his sovereign upon the matter of securing candidates of irreproachable character. "He humbly assures your Majesty that the utmost pains will be taken to provide not only for the majority but for all cases, by the strictest enquiries which the case will admit; and he has the most confident belief that the securities for character under the system, although they cannot be unerring, will be stronger and more trustworthy than any of which the present method of appointment is susceptible."

Gladstone as the sponsor of the Trevelyan-Northcote investigations naturally agreed with their report and hoped to see the government adopt its recommendations. After

[23] *Letters of Queen Victoria* (First Series) (New York, 1907), III, 12-14.

receiving the report he wrote to his colleague, Sir James Graham: "I do not want any pledges as to details; what I seek is your countenance and favour in an endeavor to introduce to the cabinet a proposal that we should give our sanction to the principle that in every case where a satisfactory test of a defined and palpable nature can be furnished, the public service shall be laid open to personal merit.... This is *my* contribution to parliamentary reform." [24]

Sir James, while believing that the change was serious and "pregnant with indirect consequences which cannot be exactly estimated or foreseen," wrote Gladstone an encouraging reply. He felt that "it will conduce to good government" and that "this proposal, if made by the Ministers of the Crown, and with the consent of the Crown, will eclipse all other reforms, and will be regarded as the greatest boon conferred on the nation since bread was freed from taxation." [25]

Lord John Russell was definitely opposed to the new merit system. Gladstone argued for it "in a letter...of incomparable trenchancy and force...," but Lord John's curt reply was, "I hope no change will be made, and I certainly must protest against it." [26]

Nevertheless, on January 26, 1854, after a long Cabinet meeting, Gladstone won his point. It is interesting to note his defense of this Cabinet later when the aristocracy had been accused of blocking the abolition of patronage. "No cabinet could have been more aristocratically composed than that over which Lord Aberdeen presided," he said. "I myself was the only one of fifteen noblemen and gentlemen who composed it, who could not fairly be said to belong to the class." [27]

[24] Lord Morley, *The Life of William Ewart Gladstone* (New York, Macmillan, 1903), I, 511.
[25] Charles Stuart Parker, *Life and Letters of Sir James Graham* (London, 1907), II, 213.
[26] Morley, *loc. cit.*
[27] *Ibid.*, pp. 511-12.

At this point the Civil Service reform movement stalled. A paragraph in the speech from the throne implied that the government was planning to introduce a bill embodying the new system, but it never appeared. The problems of the Crimean War crowded out domestic affairs, but probably the most important reason for the delay was the hostile attitude of Parliament. The members of Parliament could, with righteous smugness, abolish the patronage of the directors of the East India Company, but when it came to parting with their own valuables they found many excuses. Gladstone argued for open competition in three speeches in the House of Commons in 1855 and 1856, and when the usual cries against war-time administrative services were made he had his suggested reforms to hurl back at the critics.

But the changes which had been proposed by Trevelyan and Northcote were too much for Parliament to accept at once. The reforms they advocated have all been achieved, but the patronage fort was taken by a campaign of attrition rather than by assault. Little by little the principle of a completely nonpartisan permanent service, recruited from young men, by means of open competition in liberal studies, under the direction of a central examining body, has been adopted. The changes, with the exception of pensions, have been instituted by Orders in Council prepared by the Treasury.

To Lord Palmerston's Cabinet goes the credit for the first step. An Order in Council of May 21, 1855, established an independent board of examiners, the Civil Service Commissioners. No change was made in the method of appointment, but the Commission was to examine all candidates in tests agreed upon by the individual departments and the Commission. Each candidate had to satisfy the Commission that he was within the age limits required by the department, of good health and character, and possessed the knowledge and ability required for the position. Palmerston, "assiduous and exacting in the forms of public business," had already reconstructed the Foreign Office, and he was kindly disposed toward general improvement. But he understood the temper of Parliament, and consequently proceeded cautiously.

The Order in Council of May 21, 1855, established the Civil Service Commission as an examining board, but partisan nomination and appointment still continued. Since the examinations for each department were determined by the department head in consultation with the commissioners, the standards differed considerably, but practically all required tests in dictation, composition, arithmetic, précis, and bookkeeping. Latin, English history, and foreign languages were optional subjects. Under Labouchere the Colonial Office introduced real limited competition by weeding out the incompetents in a preliminary examination in the more simple subjects and then picking its clerks from the successful candidates in a competitive examination in classical and modern languages and literature, constitutional and international law, and mathematics. The Admiralty also had high standards, but the majority of the departments were content to appoint after candidates had been certified as passing the elementary tests. A forward step was achieved in 1859 when Parliament passed a new superannuation act, the benefits of which were limited to those entering the service with a certificate of the Civil Service Commissioners.[28] High officials, still outside the examination scheme, were exempted from the operations of the act.

During the debates on the estimates in 1860 an independent member of the House of Commons moved for a select committee to inquire into the state of the Civil Service. The Committee in examining the work of the Civil Service Commission learned that from 1855 to 1860 it had handled 10,860 nominations. In 8,039 cases only one candidate for a vacancy had been nominated. The other 2,821 persons had competed for 732 appointments. Proof that

[28] 22 Vic., c. 26.

there would be no dearth of candidates under a system of open competition was afforded by the single trial of that plan; 9 clerkships in the India Office attracted 391 competitors. During the five years the Commission granted certificates to 5,705 candidates and rejected 1,972 for failure in intellectual examinations, 343 because of age, 88 for poor health, and 76 for unsatisfactory character. In regard to those failing the educational examinations the Select Committee observed: "It is worth notice, that ... all, except 106, were rejected as deficient in arithmetic or spelling, a fact which Your Committee think ought to be borne in mind when complaints are made of the needlessly high educational requirements imposed on candidates for the Civil Service." [29]

The Committee heard evidence on the method of admission to the Civil Service, much of it favorable to open competition; but it felt that the time was not propitious for such a radical change, desiring "to avoid such precipitancy in its adoption as might possibly lead to a temporary reaction of public feeling."[30] The Committee proposed that for clerical positions there be a test to weed out the totally unfit among nominated candidates, and then a real competitive examination among at least three to five of the survivors. It was known that often in cases of limited competition two of the three competitors were "Treasury idiots" entered to simulate a contest. This was the scheme adopted by the Treasury in 1861. To nominated candidates the Civil Service Commissioners gave a preliminary examination, which included orthography, handwriting, arithmetic, composition, and bookkeeping, followed by a competitive examination in a wider range of subjects. "Wherever the new rules were accepted, there was an improvement in clerks, or at least a further elimination of the unfit. As the success of competition became more manifest, the ideal and practical advantage of

---

[29] "Report of Select Committee," *Parliamentary Papers* (1860), IX, xiv.
[30] *Ibid.*, p. vii.

patronage declined. The heads of offices could not fail to ridicule a system of patronage which introduced so many incompetents to be 'plucked' at a childish preliminary examination; and the politicians ceased to attach importance to their patronage when they could no longer insure their nominees the certainty of appointment." [31]

Indeed, within the decade following 1860 so rapidly did the value of the patronage system decline and so evident were the benefits of appointing qualified people that the Treasury could risk another forward step—the introduction of open competition for the majority of the places in the Civil Service. The significance of this step, the most important in the long line of reforms in administration, necessitates little comment. It definitely banished the patronage system; it made certain that the Civil Service would obtain employees who had demonstrated talent and potential ability under the only known system of testing them—short of a generous trial period—examinations in standard studies; and it opened an avenue of opportunity to many who were bereft of patrons or connections. The Order in Council of June 4, 1870, which introduced open competition exempted two classes of posts in the clerical service; namely, those in which appointments were made directly by the Crown, and those in which specially qualified people were appointed upon recommendation of a department head and the Treasury with certification by the Civil Service Commissioners.

In addition to introducing open competition, this Order in Council was the origin of another significant feature of the Civil Service since 1870. It divided the clerical positions into two groups. The first was to be staffed by young men who were products of the best education Britain offered. These superior officers were to be the directing brains of the administrative machine, and entrants would gradually rise to the highest permanent places in the Service. The second group was to include officers

[31] Moses, *op. cit.*, p. 127.

whose education and abilities fitted them only for the routine and less responsible duties in the departments. In other words, there was to be the great body of the clerical staff performing the routine duties of clerks, bookkeepers, and accountants, while above them would be the carefully selected *cadre* of superior officials. New classes have been introduced into the Civil Service since 1870, but the distinction between the superior and the ordinary duties of clerical officers has not been obliterated.

Treasury control over staff matters was considerably strengthened by the Order in Council of 1870. This control already existed to some degree through the Treasury's supervision of the estimates of expenditure. By this Order in Council the Treasury was empowered to approve: (1) rules framed by the Civil Service Commissioners and the departments relating to the age, health, character, and knowledge and ability of candidates for appointment; (2) examination fees; (3) dates of examinations, and vacancies and positions to be competed for; (4) additions or removals of positions on Schedule A (noncompetitive positions).

The Development of the Civil Service

The Order in Council of 1870 determined in a very general way the permanent outlines of the Service. Several extensive inquiries into the Civil Service have been made since then, but none has recommended an abandonment of the essential features of the system.

The first of the important inquiries into the Civil Service after 1870 was undertaken by a select committee of the House of Commons in 1873. Considerable dissatisfaction with the operation of the Order in Council of 1870 was being manifested, chiefly because departmental practice varied so greatly. Some of the departments adopted the scheme of two divisions while others failed to introduce the upper division clerks. Salaries and opportunities for promotion varied considerably from office to office, so that candidates entering at the same examination were soon occupying positions of glaringly unequal value.

However, the Committee of 1873 was primarily concerned with means for reducing the cost of the Service. Salaries were not unusually high, but the Committee reported that it was "impressed with the belief that in point of numbers the civil service is decidedly in excess of its requirements, and that this arises partly from the insufficient amount of work required from large numbers of permanent employees, and partly from the waste of time occasioned by employing well-educated men on merely mechanical duties." The number of redundant employees in the judicial offices was particularly large, and a greater measure of Treasury control was advocated to check this waste. The Committee recommended that the use of copying presses "should be obligatory on all public departments; and that (subject to special exceptions) no letters need be copied by hand." [32] Thus passed the chief occupation of many clerks.

Despite some very obvious faults of the Service, the early steps at reform were producing fruit. Already the character of many offices was improving, and public estimation of the government departments was higher. The genesis of that general respect and admiration for the Civil Service and public confidence in its disinterested administration is to be found at about this period. The observations of an American are evidence of this increasing confidence:

> The thorough and fearless scrutiny of the committee [of 1873] extended over several months and into every office, without respect to station, high or low—a scrutiny that brought the head of the Treasury and the Lord Chancellor to their bar, not less than the humblest clerks and doorkeepers—a scrutiny which invited and received the complaints of every discharged or discontented official who chose to appear or to write—and yet such a scrutiny did not, so far as I can discover,

[32] "Report of Select Committee," *Parliamentary Papers* (1873), Vol. VII.

disclose a single instance of peculation or fraud, nor was there any evidence or charge that illicit gains or corruption ... anywhere existed or were *by any body believed to exist in the public service*.[33]

The contrast to "the pervading venality and malversation which had prevailed in earlier generations" impressed upon Mr. Eaton the "scope and blessing of administrative reform in Great Britain." The change he attributed solely to the reforms instituted since 1855.

Unnecessary expense was not the only deficiency of the Civil Service which was complained of; so Disraeli's Conservative government when it came into power authorized a more thorough inquiry into administrative problems. The introduction of open competition had caused some dissatisfaction. Even Sir Stafford Northcote, the Chancellor of the Exchequer, now professed misgivings about the expediency of this step. Hence his cautious instructions to Dr. Lyon Playfair, the Commission's chairman.

While the Government desires as a general principle [said Sir Stafford] to uphold a system of selection according to merit, as opposed to selection by simple exercise of patronage, they are anxious that the Commission should look thoroughly into the action of the present system of competitive examinations, and should give their opinion upon any modifications which they may find it desirable to recommend in it with perfect freedom.[34]

In addition to the selection of civil servants, the Playfair Commission was to investigate the principles of transfer from office to office, grading the Service as a whole, and the employment of writers and temporary clerks.

The Playfair Report of 1875 ranks low in the list of

[33] Dorman B. Eaton, *Civil Service in Great Britain* (New York, 1880), pp. 242-43.
[34] "First Report of Playfair Commission," *Parliamentary Papers* (1875), XXIII, 4.

inquiries into the Civil Service.[35] It lacked the inspiration and courage in tackling problems that some of its predecessors and successors exhibited, and this was partly because of the equivocal attitude of the government on the new principles of public administration. A nostalgia for the days when civil servants were docile creatures of the patronage system pervades the Commission's findings.

By an Order in Council of February 12, 1876, the Treasury gave effect to some of the less contentious proposals of the Playfair Commission. The Commission had endorsed the bifurcation of the Service and proposed age limits and salary scales for the two classes. The lower division was organized along the lines proposed, but the upper division was constituted only by inference. It was referred to as a definite class of the Service, but no steps were taken to mold it along the lines of the Commission's recommendations. This anomalous condition continued for years. In 1888 a witness before the Ridley Commission declared that "the question of the universal application of the upper division of the Playfair scheme has not been considered by the Treasury for the whole service as yet." [36] Thus following the Playfair Report and the Order in Council of 1876 the Civil Service was divided into two major classes, the lower universal and definitely organized, the upper only partially applied and of indefinite constitution.

A picture of the Civil Service of more than fifty years ago has been supplied by Sir Alfred Woodgate, C.B.E., former Director of Establishments in the Ministry of Health. Sir Alfred entered the Service as a second or lower division clerk in 1879, serving in the Board of Education. He told the Tomlin Commission of 1929:

---

[35] Actually there were three reports: (1) Clerical establishments, (2) Technical branches, (3) Outdoor establishments in the Customs and Revenue departments.

[36] *Parliamentary Papers* (1888), XXVII, 2.

OLD OFFICIALDOM AND ITS REFORM 47

There is no doubt that since 1879 there has been a very great change in the Civil Service in many ways except in what one may call its structure. The structure remains very much today what it was then, excepting that the material used in the structure has been varied. Looking back to my early days, I think there is one thing that stands out: the accommodation for civil servants has improved very considerably. As regards the top of the Civil Service, the method of appointment has changed considerably. In those days, except for a few people (known as the higher division), who had come in under the Playfair Commission's report, the top consisted mainly of people appointed by patronage. When I say that let me say this also, that in my recollection that system produced some very able men; but there were some who certainly were not able men.[37]

An "extraordinary improvement" in the efficiency of the Civil Service has taken place in the past half century, according to Sir Alfred.

As regards pressure of work, in my first 10 years that certainly did not exist; my working day was usually finished, although I stayed at the office, by 2 o'clock. As regards discipline, too, today there is quite good discipline in the Public Service. In my early days, the discipline was very lax indeed. As regards efficiency, looking at the grades which would correspond today with the clerical class and the executive class, there has been an extraordinary improvement. In my early day, in 1879, and for some years after, the corresponding class to the clerical class was a class known as men copyists, and boy copyists; the men copyists were paid 10d. an hour; the boy copyists were paid 4d. an hour, and these were the successors of an earlier body of temporary clerks who used to be supplied to the Public Service by a firm called Vacher. They were the original Vacher clerks of the sixties. The work was farmed out, and that class was an extraordinary class; it had among it some quite brilliant men; it also had among it the most Bohemian set of people one could ever imagine. It was no

[37] *Royal Commission on the Civil Service, 1929-31, Minutes of Evidence,* Q. 22,187.

uncommon thing for them to work, for instance, with a jug of beer under their chairs, and that sort of thing.

With regard to the work itself, any work bordering on responsibility in any shape or form never came down to the clerks at all. No clerk, even one getting £300 or £400 a year, had authority in those days to send out a form, unless it had been initialled or authorized by one of the higher staff. In addition to that an extraordinary amount of work was done which, looking back, one can see was absolutely waste of time. For the first 10 years of my service I was occupied in copying entries out of one book into another book. All that work has long since been swept away. There was no delegation in those days at all, and there were no women in the Civil Service except the charwomen....

Then there is one other thing which... should be mentioned, and that is the extraordinary sanctity of the Permanent Secretary in those days to the ordinary clerical staff. He was a sort of Mikado. I served in the Education Department, for I think 5 years, while the late Lord Sandford was secretary; I never saw him once, and I do not think any other clerk saw him unless he misbehaved himself. But that has changed; today, so far as his other duties permit, the Permanent Secretary of a Department endeavours to know his staff. That has been a good change....[38]

A little more than a decade after the Playfair Report another intensive inquiry into the state of the Civil Service was instituted. A commission under the chairmanship of Sir Matthew White Ridley was empowered "to inquire into the numbers, salaries, hours of labour, superannuation, cost of the staff, and the administration, regulation, and organisation of the said offices." [39] The Commission also was to report on the efficiency of departments and the results of the Playfair scheme of organization. The second report was devoted to the or-

[38] *Ibid.*, Q. 21,188.
[39] "First Report of Royal Commission on the Civil Service," *Parliamentary Papers* (1887), Vol. XIX. The Commission issued four reports found in *Parliamentary Papers*, 1887, Vol. XIX; 1888, Vol. XXVII; 1889, Vol. XXI; 1890, Vol. XXVII.

ganization and efficiency of the general clerical staff of the Service.

In the Playfair Report there was some skepticism about open competition as a ruling principle, but none of that existed in the conclusions of the Ridley Commission. This body found that the division of the Civil Service into two major classes had "the sanction of almost every experienced administrator," and accordingly it recommended the continuation, with certain changes, of this bifurcated system.

The highest administrative work of the Service was to be performed by the First Division, a class of more definite constitution than the Upper or Higher Division which existed in a rather nebulous state after the Playfair Report. Its numbers were to be smaller than the existing Upper Division, for the Commission discovered many clerks of the latter class performing duties of an inferior sort. Young men were to compete in examinations of university caliber for these posts, and salaries in the three grades of the First Division were to range from a minimum of £200 to a maximum of £1,000.

The bulk of the clerical work in government departments should be performed, in the Commission's opinion, by the class established after the Playfair Report as the Lower Division—the name to be changed to Second Division to satisfy the sensibilities of the staff. The character of the entrance examination, the standard of remuneration, and the quality of clerks employed gained the general approval of the Ridley Commissioners. Discovering that "routine promotion by seniority is the great evil of the Service," the Ridley Commission declared that "it is indispensable to proceed ... strictly on the principle of promotion by merit, that is to say, selecting always the fittest man, instead of considering claims in order of seniority, and rejecting only the unfit." Evidently with the abolition of the "pull" of patrons there had been a swing to the opposite extreme, advancement by seniority alone; and the latter was only slightly less fatal to efficiency than the other, for ambition and initiative soon wilt in such an atmosphere.

The next grand inquisition into Civil Service problems was undertaken during the years 1912-15 by a Royal Commission under the chairmanship of Lord MacDonnell. During the more than twenty years intervening between the Ridley and MacDonnell inquiries important changes occurred in the Civil Service, so that the MacDonnell Commission not only had to consider some of the old problems but a number of new ones. For one thing, a new class had been created in the clerical corps. This Intermediate Clerical Class, 1,400 strong in 1914, was recruited from boys eighteen or nineteen years of age with a public school education and occupied a position between the First and Second Divisions. Introduced in the Admiralty, it was created to perform work requiring an education superior to that found among Second Division clerks but still not as high as the caliber of Division I. The Intermediate Class was extended to several other departments where a demand for such clerks existed. Between the Second Division and the Boy Copyists there had been introduced a class known as the Assistant Clerks or Abstractor Class, recruited from Boy Clerks between the ages of seventeen and eighteen. These clerks performed copying and other routine work under direct supervision, and provided a necessary group of trained, established civil servants for duties inferior to those committed to the Second Division clerks.

In conformity with the recommendations of the Ridley Commission, the First Division had been reduced in numbers, partly through the substitution of Intermediate Clerks. In 1914 it numbered about 700. The employment of women, a novelty when the Ridley Commission reported, had been gradually extended. The Post Office was the largest employer of women clerks, but female typists were recognized as a class common to the Service in 1894 and they were used in a number of departments.

Another change was the increasing employment of technical experts of various sorts. As the state extended its paternalistic arm, and it did so very rapidly in the early years of the twentieth century, these experts became essential to the management of many services. Engineers, chemists, doctors, and lawyers were added in increasing numbers. New problems of recruitment and organization were thereupon introduced. The customary system of nontechnical examinations for young men leaving school or university was unsuited to the recruitment of experts. The state naturally desired men of professional training and some practical experience, and hence they had to be taken at older ages than the ordinary entrants and paid commensurate salaries. The place of the professional or technical expert in the departmental organization raised perplexing problems. The British plan has always been to use the expert as the adviser of the layman in whose hands rests the final authority, but this traditional system did not function so smoothly when specialists were introduced into organizations staffed with administrative experts. It frequently is the nature of experts to disagree, and the high priests of the new sciences looming so large in state services were unwilling to have their advice filtered through the ordinary departmental authorities. The extensive employment of experts also presented the problem of their promotion within departments and consideration for high administrative positions. A conflict of interests with the First Division Brahmins was inevitable.

Paternalism and the extension of public ownership multiplied the numbers of the Civil Service. For example, the nationalization of the telephones on January 1, 1912, added 18,000 employees to the state. Most of these employees formed classes outside the regular clerical service, and there immediately arose vital questions concerning their relationship to the state. Did they succeed to the various privileges of civil servants and did they lose their right of striking which they possessed against private employers? It is evident, therefore, that the MacDonnell Commission faced a Civil Service considerably transformed and bearing within its growing body problems of extreme complexity and gravity.

The Royal Commission under the chairmanship of Lord MacDonnell was an exceptionally able one. Leaders in the political and intellectual life of Great Britain were included within the membership, some of whom were destined to be prominent in public affairs for many years to come.[40] Of the Commission's methods and personnel a contemporary observer wrote:

> In keeping with the spirit of the age, this inquiry is conducted in a manner at once scientific, open-minded, and sympathetic. The new sociology, the new democracy, and the advanced ideals of national education are evident in cross examinations which are no longer painstaking and perfunctory. The commission is, we may say, a conservative one, in that the majority belong to the upper, highly-educated class of administrators, university professors, and members of Parliament—but there has been a noticeable disposition on the part of the whole commission to bring the civil service into line with modern needs, and to look upon new experiments without shuddering.[41]

For two years the Commission heard testimony and gathered evidence before preparing the reports issued. On the whole, the Commission endorsed the lines of development of the Service up to that time, but it had some important changes to suggest. It recommended a closer integration of the Civil Service recruitment policy with

---

[40] Besides Lord MacDonnell, the members of the Royal Commission were: the Duke of Devonshire, the Bishop of Southwark, Sir Kenneth Augustus Muir Mackenzie, K.C.B., Sir Henry Primrose, K.C.B., C.S.I., Sir Donald MacAlister, K.C.B., Sir William Guy Granet, Harold Trevor Baker, Alfred Allen Booth, Arthur Boutwood, John Robert Clynes, Samuel John Gurney Hoare, Richard Durning Holt, Percy Ewing Matheson, Arthur Everett Shipley, Philip Snowden, Graham Wallas, Elizabeth Sanderson Haldane, and Lucy Anne Evelyn.

[41] Moses, *op. cit.*, pp. 183-84.

OLD OFFICIALDOM AND ITS REFORM 53

the educational system, so that the ages for entering the various government departments would correspond with the ages at which young men and women left schools. It suggested a greater measure of Treasury control with a special section within that department to exercise this supervision. On the question of female civil servants the Commission summarized its position by stating, "The principle governing the employment of women should be to secure the advantage of the services of women whenever those services will best promote the public interest." [42]

It found that more women could be employed advantageously, especially as typists. The Commission penned several guarded statements regarding the political and syndicalist activities of civil servants and admonished them to observe "a proper reserve and reticence both in speech and writing" in respect to political questions.[43] A large share of the work of this competent Commission was rendered useless by the World War, but its opinions and advice on recurring problems of administration justify the effort expended.

The third Royal Commission to survey the Civil Service was appointed in 1929. Lord Tomlin was its chairman, and all three political parties contributed to its not too outstanding membership.[44] After hearing a great deal of evidence from public officers, Civil Service

[42] Cmd. 7338 (1914), p. 107. The MacDonnell Commission issued six reports. The first three were progress reports; the fourth (Cmd. 7338, 1914) dealt with the administrative and clerical staffs; the fifth (Cmd. 7748, 1914), the Diplomatic and Consular Services; the sixth (Cmd. 7832, 1915), the Legal Departments. The *Minutes of Evidence* were issued as appendices to the reports.

[43] *Ibid.*, p. 97.

[44] The members of the Royal Commission were: Lord Tomlin, the Duchess of Atholl, Sir Christopher Thomas Needham, Sir Henry Sharp, Sir Percy Richard Jackson, Sir Assheton Pownall, James Black Baillie, William Cash, Frank Walter Goldstone, Barbara Ayrton Gould, Mary Agnes Hamilton, Eveline Mary Lowe, Thomas Ellis Naylor, Percy John Pybus, Robert Richards, and Margaret Wintringham. Mr. Naylor resigned, and John Bromley was appointed.

associations, civic organizations, business men, and educational authorities, the Commission submitted its report in 1931.

"Since 1914," the Tomlin Commission reported, "the Service has undergone considerable change. Its functions have been extended, the position of women has been altered materially and new methods of wage negotiation have been introduced. Further, the war resulted in a dislocation of normal methods of recruitment which have not yet been fully restored." [45]

Despite this admission that it was faced with quite important developments in the field of public administration, the Commission failed to seize the opportunity to prepare an outstanding report. Its report reads like an excursion of the Treasury into self-analysis. There is a little censure, considerable criticism, and a fair share of proposing, but in the end the Commission concludes that things are about right as they are.

Lest this seem unreasonably hard on the Royal Commission these points in extenuation of its attitude can be recorded. The British Civil Service is, comparatively measured, a fine administrative organization, so some of the grosser evils one might expect to uncover in even the progressive nations are absent here. The case for the merit system has been proved, and all sections of opinion are agreed on the general idea of a nonpartisan, career service. The Tomlin Commission, therefore, did not need to take a stand for merit against patronage; the great battles in that field have been won. Another point in the Commission's defense is that the Service underwent a great deal of renovating just after the War, and in 1930 it was too soon to see whether these changes were satisfactory or not. There is much to be said for the Commission's position that "at the present time in particular there is special need for caution. The material on which to judge the

[45] Cmd. 3909 (1931), *Report of the Royal Commission on the Civil Service, 1929-31*, p. 5.

existing organisation is meagre."[46] Constant tinkering with an organization like the Civil Service can scarcely be beneficial. And finally, the Royal Commission was forced to bear in mind the parlous state of the nation's finances. The unlikelihood of any government's increasing the cost of the Civil Service tempered the Commission's report and probably made it more cautious than it would have been in times of relative prosperity.

With due regard paid to these limiting factors, the Tomlin Commission's report was disappointing. It reads like an elaborate description of the mechanics of a motor car which never mentions that this is a vehicle with uses which are highly important in the life of the modern world. The Civil Service is related at many points to the social changes which have been going on in England for half a century, but very little of this fact is gleaned from the Commission's study. Some of the problems which arise from this changing context will be discussed in later chapters.

However, a few problems studied by the Commission may be mentioned at this point. The Commission endorsed the classification of the Civil Service as it now exists. The most important issue in this connection is whether the uniformity of classification introduced in 1920, after the study and report of the Reorganisation Committee of the National Whitley Council, has proceeded far enough, for a large proportion of the clerical employees are still in departmental classes.[47] Staff organizations are strongly of the opinion that there is no justification for the continuance of these departmental classes and that they are retained because of their relative cheapness.[48] The Commission, nevertheless, bowed to official opinion and declared,

---

[46] *Ibid.,* p. 10.
[47] There are approximately 20,000 officers in the Treasury Clerical Class and 16,000 in the departmental classes.
[48] *Royal Commission on the Civil Service, 1929-31, Minutes of Evidence,* App. XV, par. 136, Q. 4,970-74.

"In our view, speaking generally, uniformity in organisation and grading cannot be carried any further in the Service than at present." [49]

The Commission found "the present general standard of remuneration... reasonable in the light of the wage levels now prevailing...." [50] It recommended the substitution of consolidated wage and salary scales for the plan of basic pay plus cost of living bonus which had been introduced during the World War when sharply rising prices threw the whole remuneration system out of adjustment. After much negotiating between the Treasury and the staff associations, consolidation was achieved in 1934.

The staff classified as "professional, scientific and technical" has grown rapidly as the state has assumed new service functions. In 1930 there were approximately 22,000 officers, or 7 per cent of the nonindustrial staff of the Civil Service, so classified.[51] This staff has been added on a departmental basis, and "more than 500 distinct grades" have resulted. Some simplification is desirable, but the Commission did not have much to offer besides Treasury and departmental study of the problem. The higher specialists do not regard their position vis à vis ministers and Administrative Class officers as completely satisfactory. They complain that they are not always consulted on technical matters and that their advice reaches the ministers through the sieve of the nonspecialist staff. This would appear to be a problem for ministers and permanent secretaries to work out, and as the Commission observed, "a standard code" cannot be prescribed.[52]

The extensive employment of women in the Civil Service is a relatively recent problem. During and after the War they were recruited in large numbers, and at present there

[49] Cmd. 3909 (1931), p. 44.
[50] *Ibid.*, p. 87.
[51] *Ibid.*, p. 49.
[52] *Ibid.*, p. 51.

OLD OFFICIALDOM AND ITS REFORM 57

are approximately 80,000 in the Civil Service.[53] The sex issue in the Service may be summarized under two demands, equal opportunity and equal pay. As a result of the Sex Disqualification (Removal) Act of 1919, and resolutions in the House of Commons, the former has practically been achieved in principle, and the Royal Commission's recommendation was for general adherence to the policy of "fair field and no favour." [54] The nature of the work requires that some positions be reserved for men and remnants of masculine prejudice rule out women in a few other instances.[55] "We are divided almost equally," the Commission confessed in regard to equal pay.[56] The Treasury and the government have not budged from their position of opposition.[57] Women civil servants continue to receive, therefore, approximately 75 to 80 per cent of the remuneration of male officers of the same grade and class.

Established civil servants upon retirement receive pensions under a noncontributory, gratuitous system established by a long series of Superannuation Acts.[58] A civil servant is eligible for a pension at the age of sixty or upon

[53] In 1929 the figure was 79,022.—"Treasury Memoranda," *Royal Commission on the Civil Service, 1929-31,* p. 223.

[54] Cmd. 3909 (1931), p. 115.

[55] The exclusion of women from the Diplomatic Service is a sore point with many feminists. The Royal Commission passed the problem back to the government as raising "issues of high policy." An interdepartmental committee has disposed of the question for the time being by continuing their exclusion. In a White Paper the view was expressed that "the time had not come for their employment in the diplomatic or consular service with advantage to the State or profit to women."—*The New York Times,* April 29, 1936.

[56] Cmd. 3909 (1931), p. 131.

[57] On April 1, 1936, the Labor Opposition carried a motion introduced by Miss Ellen Wilkinson to pay women civil servants the same salaries as men. Upon reconsideration the government won 149 to 134. The majority was small because few M.P.'s like to vote against equal pay.—*The New York Times,* April 2, 1936.

[58] Eligibility for pensions is the principal distinction between established and unestablished civil servants. Established civil servants comprise a little more than 50 per cent of the Service. About one-third of the unestablished employees are part-time staff.—"Treasury Memoranda," *Royal Commission on the Civil Service, 1929-31,* pp. 3-4.

a breakdown in health. The annual pension amounts to 1/80 of salary for each year of service, subject to a maximum of 40/80. A lump sum allowance of 1/30 of salary for each year of service, subject to a maximum of 45/30, is given each civil servant upon retirement. In view of the considerable dissatisfaction among the staff with the present system, the Commission recommended the introduction of a contributory scheme, and the inclusion of some 152,000 unpensionable employees (largely industrial staff, porters, etc.) within the new system.[59] No action, however, has been taken on this recommendation. The Treasury feels that the present scheme induces civil servants to remain in the Service for a life career, but at the same time it forces some to stay who are dissatisfied and who injure the *esprit de corps* of the staff. The state pays out more than £7,000,000 annually in Civil Service pensions.

These are a few of the important issues reviewed by the Tomlin Commission. Others will be referred to in subsequent chapters. In a growing institution like the Civil Service problems are constantly arising, and the work of adjustment is never completed.

[59] Cmd. 3909 (1931), pp. 201 ff.

CHAPTER III

The Honorable Member

A YOUNG journalist once approached the chief Liberal whip of the House of Commons to inquire about a dispute over the adoption of a candidate in a Scottish constituency. The whip suggested that the twenty-four-year-old journalist offer himself as a candidate to the divided Liberals of the district. When he demurred because he lacked the train fare to reach the constituency, the whip assured him that this matter could be arranged without difficulty. By midnight he was on his way to Scotland, and a few days later he was back at Westminster as the member for Kirkcaldy Burghs. Such is the way the late Lord Dalziel told the story of his entrance into the House of Commons in 1892.

Since the disappearance of the pocket boroughs of pre-Reform days not many young men can expect such rapid and fortuitous entrances into the popular house of Parliament. Most of them must climb rather steep paths before they can write "M.P." after their names. Were some mentor to provide a regimen for politically ambitious young Englishmen, after the fashion of the guides for princes, popular in Machiavellian days, he would have to include instructions for hurdling a good many obstacles standing between desire and realization. Simply advising young men to approach party whips with the expectation of being requested to stand in a fairly safe constituency would not recommend the guide very widely.

Should anyone consider it worth his while to prepare such a guide for young Americans aspiring to seats in

Congress, his advice would probably run something like this. Obtain a law degree from one of the many institutions willing to confer this honor. Open an office or enter a firm in a town of a Congressional district not unalterably opposed to your political persuasion. "Join" everything, enter actively into the work of the local party organization, and hope for the nomination as county prosecutor or state's attorney. After a few years of faithful party service, during which time you have acquired a local reputation in or out of office, you may aspire to the nomination for the House of Representatives, and if it is a good year for your party you may win. From then on it is largely a matter of picking loyal postmasters and obtaining your share from the national pork barrel. This advice would serve for either party, since the small town lawyer seems to be the typical Congressman, Democrat or Republican.

Outlining the career and drawing a picture of the typical M.P. is not so simple as in the American case, although it must not be supposed that Metropolitan New York and the Iowa cornfields elect identical types to Congress. There is plenty of difference between a Tammany protégé and a son of the prairie or the Mississippi bayous, but still the inhabitants of Capitol Hill run sufficiently to type to be easily recognized in the cartoons.

There used to be a standardized type in the House of Commons—so true was this that an historian can write that until the general election of 1906 an eighteenth-century member of Parliament could have returned and catalogued the politicians he found at Westminster with a fair degree of accuracy, for they had changed little since his day. Dress the member of 1900 in the wigs and lace of 1800, and a long step in turning the clock back a century would have been taken.

This type is common in the Conservative party today, which means that the governing classes of yore still occupy seats in Parliament regardless of how wide the franchise is distributed. In picturing a typical representative of the governing classes you must start with the family. It must be one with social prestige and roots deep in the life of some community—one with portraits of ancestors to gaze upon. Conservative voters of all classes apparently like Parliamentary candidates from families that have traditionally participated in politics. A scion of a noble family, providing that he is personally attractive, appeals to the twentieth-century electorate just as he appealed to the eighteenth, and the presence of twenty-seven Conservative members in the last Parliament who were the sons of peers, most of them heirs to the title, substantiates this. Of course, they have the assistance of wealth and influential connections in getting into the House of Commons, but nevertheless they have in addition a strong popular appeal in name and tradition. Besides scions of the nobility there are numerous representatives of old county families who even look with disdain upon the slightly parvenu Georgian and Victorian peerage. A son of the "beerage" rates nothing in the eyes of a twenty-sixth baronet. And these old county families fill many a seat on the green benches at Westminster.

The typical member from the governing classes will have his family background supported by an education at the seats of learning which his ancestors have attended for generations. Almost half (218) of the approximately 460 Conservative members of the House of Commons before the general election of 1935 attended one of the public schools of England, and a reunion of old Etonians would bring together no less than eighty-nine members. Harrow, Rugby, and Winchester follow along with substantial quotas. From a public school our typical member will have gone to either Oxford or Cambridge. Two hundred and one of the last Conservative majority in Parliament attended one of the two great universities. Trinity College, Cambridge, was the preferred choice, claiming thirty-eight members, while "the House," Christ Church,

Oxford, sheltered twenty-seven. Many who did not go up to the Universities entered the Army or Royal Navy, and the Conservative party in the Commons had some eighty-four members who had held commissions in one of the armed services. A number of others served in the fighting forces during the World War but did not belong to the Sandhurst type of professional soldier.

If our young man must seek his fortune in the world, he will quite probably turn to the law. That eternal and world-wide affinity between politics and law is demonstrated in English public life where the lawyers far outnumber all other professions. Eighty-three Conservative M.P.'s were members of the legal profession.

This then is our Conservative member who follows in the tradition of the eighteenth and nineteenth centuries. He comes from a socially-elect family, probably prominent in English public life for many generations. He goes to a public school and then to the "varsity" or one of the military colleges. He may be called to the bar or serve a term with the Guards; but at an early age he enters politics and, supported by name, wealth, and connections, he is soon in the House of Commons.

This type of Conservative must share his party with one who is a son of the commercial world. The latter comes from the upper middle classes, made wealthy or prominent, often both, by manufacturing, trade, or banking. For more than a century he has been finding a place among the governing classes, and between the newest business successes and the oldest aristocratic families there are an infinite number of gradations. The successful business man's tendency is to buy a country seat and live the life of a squire, while the older families find the marts of trade a necessary place to earn the wealth their position demands. And so all avenues of social rank tend to lead into one square where the traffic intermingles. The history of Sir Robert Peel's family has been re-enacted time after time. His father, a successful pioneer of the Industrial

Revolution, a calico printer, set himself up as a country gentleman, entered politics, and introduced his son to a political career which led him to the premiership. The Liberal party used to be the political home of most of this commercial aristocracy, and for three-quarters of a century after the Act of 1832 admitted them to the councils of state they ruled the Whig fort. But while the Liberal philosophers after the War hunted for some middle ground between right and left, many of the business community deserted to the Conservative side where the dogma was simple even if the practice occasionally was compromising. So today there is added to the Tory nobility and squirearchy the City element, the captains of industry. Usually their entrance into public life must wait the achievement of business success, but that gives them wealth and reputation to assist their ambition.

The Liberal party, perennially bifurcated since the World War, was divided into two wings during the National government's ascendancy. The National Liberals were part of the tricephalous government inaugurated in 1931; the other Liberals (including the Lloyd Georgian ménage of four Independent Liberals), finally unable to stomach protection and Ottawa, went their way in opposition. Their numbers were almost equal, thirty-five and thirty-six respectively. Habit and tradition, and also perhaps some belief in the magic of free trade, have prevented all the elements which once made the Liberals the business men's party from scampering off to the Conservative shelter. In fact, the business men and the lawyers dominate both wings of the party.

Only a small fraction, nine out of seventy-one, of the Liberal Parliamentarians in the last House of Commons were public school products, but twenty-four attended Oxford or Cambridge. Eighteen attended other British universities, many of them their native institutions north of the Tweed. The old Whig aristocracy has almost entirely disappeared from the Liberal party in the House of Commons, and only two heirs of peers sat under the old label. The absence of the high social classes is also to be noted in the fact that only two Liberal M.P.'s came to the House of Commons from the armed services while the Conservative benches swarmed with retired officers of all ranks. Their names are less noticeable, too, on the rosters of the fashionable and exclusive London clubs. Whereas such clubs as the Bath, Boodle's, the Marlborough, and White's have a goodly number of Conservative M.P.'s, the Liberal members are very rare.

Anyone aspiring to be a Labor M.P. could ask for nothing better, so it would seem, than to have been forced to enter the coal mines as a boy, for from this humble start no less than twenty-five of the fifty-eight members of the last House had literally risen from the ground up. All of them had climbed through trade union circles until they had sufficient prestige with their fellow workmen to secure a seat in Parliament. Coal miners from Wales, Durham, and Scotland formed the backbone of the Labor opposition to the National government in the House of Commons, but they had the support of a number of other trade union representatives—officials of various labor organizations. Altogether thirty-three past or present trade union officials sat as Labor members at Westminster. The high proportion of miners in the Labor Opposition before the election of 1935 is not likely to be typical, and it is considerably less in the present House. A substantial proportion of Labor Parliamentarians has served an apprenticeship in local government office. This entering of national politics through a borough or county council is common in all three parties, but it is particularly so in the Labor party. Frequently as the chairmen of important local government committees young men have demonstrated capacity for activity in larger fields. In passing it should be noted that, despite the sweeping defeats in the general elections of 1931 and 1935, Labor's hold on many local governments has not been disturbed.

While the general election of 1935 made changes in the number of members belonging to the political parties in the House of Commons, it did not effect any revolution in the personnel of that chamber. After the election the government had 428 members divided as follows: Conservatives, 387; Simonite Liberals, 33; National Laborites, 8. The opposition was composed of: Labor, 154; Independent Liberals, 21; Independent Labor Party, 4; Communist Party, 1. The postelection personnel of the two chief parties has been characterized by Professor Laski in these words:

> In the government parties, the three main groups by occupation will be rentiers (the largest group), business men, and barristers; and there is one ex-working man in the Conservative Party. Forty-five members of the parties are either holders of hereditary titles or their sons; and over one-quarter of the party was educated at the single school of Eton. Predominately and notably, that is to say, the Government side of the House is a representative sample of the upper class in the community.
>
> The Labour Party is almost exactly divided in representation. Half its members are trade unionists, 34 of these being miners, and half belonging to other trades and professions. Dr. Addison apart, many of its representatives who were in the 1929 government were re-elected. But it remains an outstanding feature of the party that few of its young "intellectuals" were returned, and it is, relatively speaking, of a high average age compared with its rivals.[1]

The trade union element constitutes a sort of Labor party governing class, which causes some sympathizers who wish to see the party erected on a broader social base to feel that able young men do not get an opportunity in the party because of the preponderant voice of the unionists. Be that as it may, the trade unionists can point out that but for their backlog of strength, particularly in the min-

---

[1] Harold J. Laski, "The General Election, 1935," *The Political Quarterly,* January-March, 1936, p. 2.

ing areas, the Parliamentary Labor party would virtually have been swept out of existence in the general election of 1931. Probably as the pioneers of the Labor party movement pass on the torch to younger followers it will be to men with more formal education and from more heterogeneous backgrounds than the present members, for the sons of miners and mechanics are going to universities on scholarships and are entering the professions. Even the small group of Labor peers might be expected to sire some future leaders, except for a policy of honoring childless politicians. The older men have demonstrated that while the House of Commons may be the finest club in London its doors can be passed by men without name, wealth, or formal schooling. One whose life was a proof of this wrote:

It used to be said that the better-to-do classes with roots in the country and incomes of an assured character dedicated their offspring to the public service one after the other—one to inherit the property and do the work of the squire either on the bench or in the shooting coverts, another to enter the Church, another to represent the pocket borough in the House of Commons. That was "in the old days," and the world has changed. There is now no class that holds a prerogative to govern; there is now no service earmarked for any social group. In the school knapsack of every youth may be hidden the title of a Privy Councillor, in his clothes box the gold lace of a Minister of State.[2]

Seeking to reduce the courses to a Parliamentary career to a few well-fenced highways would be very misleading, for every member represents an individual variation of some kind. The personal equation enters into all their careers. The scion of the noblest family in Britain might find it impossible in these democratic days to win a seat in the House of Commons if he lacked the personal qualities demanded of a candidate, and not every general sec-

[2] J. Ramsay MacDonald, *op. cit.*, p. 101.

retary of a labor union can take to the hustings and win a poll. A veteran M.P. said once, "I have never ceased to wonder why some people, apparently endowed with every necessary quality, never can get into the House, whereas others apparently far more slenderly equipped with brains and the faculty of using them, simply push the door open on oiled hinges.... There is just a something, a personality, a touch of sympathy, a measure of personal charm which outweighs the more solid qualities of the other." [3]

Several features of a young man's personal equipment or events of his early career appear to be of definite advantage in gaining a seat in the House of Commons under any party label. One is the ability to address somewhat noisy and critical political gatherings. The English practice of heckling puts a premium upon quick thinking and pointed speaking that is quite unknown in countries where the politicians deliver prepared addresses to audiences that only respond by applause or hisses. A candidate must dominate his audience and turn every verbal missile into a boomerang upon the head of his critic. As an illustration of one technique, there is a story about Sir Edward Marshall-Hall, a noted barrister and former M.P. who died a few years ago. While he was addressing a political meeting he got into deep water in explaining his position on agricultural policy. A heckler shouted at him, "What about oats?" "Stand up, my good man," Sir Edward replied. Then quickly, "Oh, I am sorry. I only saw two legs before."

Not all speakers can fire back so pointedly, and some of course rely upon erudition or deep sincerity rather than the clever retort to conquer their audiences. But political speaking in England is conducted in a more rough and tumble style than in the United States, and winning a trick of word play counts for more. A debate between

---

[3] Robert Farquharson, *The House of Commons from Within* (London, 1912), p. 51.

American and English collegians is an interesting contrast of styles. The Americans attempt to win by the irrefutable logic of their argument, heightening interest once in a while by a carefully selected bit of humor or a well-drawn analogy. The English, on the other hand, try to capture their listeners by rattling off a familiar essay on the topic of the debate or showing up the absurdity of their opponents' position. The result is usually ludicrous. To a limited degree—quite limited since there is plenty of serious speech-making in English campaigns—political speaking in the two countries is analogous to their debating styles. That is to say, in Britain clever debating skill seems more important than the ability to deliver a polished address from a prepared manuscript.

Perhaps the necessity of forensic skill explains the fact that election to the presidency of the Union at Oxford University is almost certain assurance of getting into the House of Commons. No less than ten former presidents of the Oxford Union and three of the Cambridge Union were members of the last Parliament. Besides the speaking ability which presiding over these debating societies requires, these young men are assisted by an acquaintance with the leading political figures of the day, because of the politicians' practice of regularly defending their policies and beliefs before the University undergraduates. A career in Parliament is almost immediately open to these gifted young men.

Acquaintanceship with prominent politicians and the establishment of highly useful connections come about in another way that is common in British public life. That is the practice of a politically ambitious young man serving as a private secretary to some leading statesman, and it is a piece of particularly good luck for one who does not possess a famous name or connections which would bring him to the attention of party leaders at once. The House of Commons contains a score or more of members who have "devilled" at some time for a minister or prominent opposition leader. Former private secretaries of Lloyd George, Winston Churchill, Stanley Baldwin, and other well-known statesmen dot the benches at Westminster. Introduced at once into the circle of the leading politicians of the day, these young men are frequently invited to contest constituencies where no local candidate is available. While some of these are forlorn hopes, some others are good opportunities to win a seat or to make such a fine impression that they are slated for a better chance soon. The grooming of young candidates which the whips and the central offices of British parties undertake is important in opening up opportunities for fresh figures in political life at Westminster. It helps if the candidate has a few thousand pounds to expend on his career, for constituencies are always receptive to a personally financed candidate, but even this is not essential if the young man obviously has talent. British voters are not so parochially-minded that they insist upon local candidates, so opportunities are constantly appearing for the forwarding of a promising man by the party's general staff.

A more exclusive preserve than the House of Commons is the Cabinet. Every textbook on British government describes how a prime minister selects his colleagues and what factors he must bear in mind in order to construct a harmonious official family. Not so frequently is observed the extent to which the so-called professional politicians monopolize the Cabinet.[4] Ministerial office almost invariably goes to a man who has made politics his career from youth, and only occasionally does a person who has entered Parliament at the age of forty or later ever win a Cabinet post. This doesn't mean that a young man has no opportunity of getting within the select circle, but he

[4] Data on the occupations of cabinet ministers bear this out. Professor Laski has shown that "the distribution of occupations among the parents of cabinet ministers is wider than among the ministers themselves."—"The Personnel of the English Cabinet, 1801-1924," *The American Political Science Review*, February, 1928, p. 24.

must start early and usually have some recommendation which brings him to the attention of his elders. These recommendations are both those of lineage and personality. The scions of politically influential families have an early claim on Cabinet posts, and Cecils, Cavendishes, and Russells keep reappearing on the Front Bench.[5] The son of a prominent political figure has a long start on his Parliamentary colleagues. Herbert Gladstone a generation ago and Malcolm MacDonald today illustrate this sort of nepotism. A brilliant scholar from Oxford or Cambridge, a Union president, or even a rowing or cricket blue has a fame that he may capitalize upon. Then there are a few members of every Cabinet who by watching the signs along the route and avoiding attractive by-paths of political heresy or radicalism have trudged a well-worn road to the Cabinet room. The conventional route is set forth in the following account:

The Minister was a man just past the middle term of life. His education had been of the conventional kind. From a fashionable school he had proceeded to Cambridge where his career had been respectable and industrious. He had been called to the Bar, but his voice was heard more often at public meetings than in the Courts of Justice. Possessing some local influence his father had secured his election for a borough with a consistent record of party attachment, and at his death had endowed him with a patrimony sufficient to meet the expense of a place in the country, a house in London during the Parliamentary season, and a constituency which was satisfied with a modest subscription list and a reasonable number of dinners and bazaars. As a private member he put on harness of the approved pattern and was docile in the shafts. He had prudently abstained from the cabals of Jacobins below the gangway and from the *carbonari* of the smoking-room, and he never spoke when he was asked to be silent. Constant in the lobby and obliging on the platform he became an established favourite with the Whips who admitted him to the select

[5] "Aristocrats ... enter the House of Commons and the cabinet ten years earlier, on the average, than commoners."—*Ibid.*, p. 26.

coterie of visitors to their room, where cigarettes are smoked and claims to promotion are examined. As he had displayed some readiness in the class of speech which is wanted in the dinner-hour or on occasions when a necessary debate is languishing, he was rewarded by an appointment to an Under-Secretaryship.[6]

After a season in opposition our hero re-enters office as a member of the Cabinet, and as long as he remains active in politics and *persona grata* to the party, prime ministers must recognize his claims.

It seems essential that a member start early if he is to wear the gold braid of a minister of state, for those that do form a trust which is rarely open to a late arrival. British politics of the nineteenth century was pretty much monopolized by these long-term professionals. Peel, Palmerston, Lord John Russell, Disraeli, all were veterans of many years, and of course Gladstone's more than three score years in public life top them all. Playfair is once said to have complained to the Grand Old Man about being left out of a Cabinet. "You are too old for office," Gladstone replied.

"But, sir, I am much younger than you."

"That may be, but I am an exception to all rules."

As a matter of fact, he was only proving the rule. As the dean of the Commoners he had an unshakeable position in the Liberal party. The Labor party has followed in the tradition of its rivals, and its two Cabinets have been the hoariest of all. MacDonald, Snowden, Thomas, Lansbury, Henderson, and the rest were veteran professionals like their Conservative and Liberal opponents.

The United States is looked upon as the happy hunting ground of the professional politicians, and undoubtedly more people here are deriving their bread and butter, and a good deal of jam besides, from serving the public than anywhere else; but still a great proportion of the Americans holding high political office come from private life,

[6] *Studies of Yesterday,* by a Privy Councillor (London, 1928), pp. 3, 4.

and their official careers are interludes in their more normal lives. There are no American figures of the nineteenth century who dominate political life as do some of their English contemporaries. In the twentieth century the two Roosevelts and Coolidge were professional politicians in the English sense, and Taft and Harding should perhaps be included. But the Princeton schoolmaster and the Palo Alto engineer had had successful careers in private life before politics beckoned. During these years British prime ministers have all been veteran politicians whose only careers have been in Parliament. The constitutional systems of the two countries affect this phenomenon, of course, but nevertheless American politics, despite party wheel-horses, Old Guards, and machines, is a far more open game.

A curious feature of English public life is that these men of Cabinet rank appear as lifelong amateurs while at the same time performing as professionals. Most of them give the impression that politics is a sort of avocation to which they are drawn by a desire to be of service or to champion a cause close to their hearts. There have been examples of men conscripted by a high sense of duty to a public life, but for most of them, it is ventured, the obligation is an intoxicating pleasure which is essential to their lives. The late Earl Grey is said to have entered politics under pressure, and during his career he quite sincerely seemed to long more for the company of his birds and rustic haunts than for that of diplomats and political colleagues; but probably the nostalgia for the quiet life was more genuine in his case than most.

Today Lord Baldwin is the supreme example of this layman caught up by high political office. As Professor Laski has said, "He has the Englishman's genius for appearing an amateur in a game in which, in fact, he is a superb professional." [7] And what a capital asset it is! "Everyone

[7] Harold J. Laski, "Britain's Baldwin," *Current History*, August, 1935, p. 458.

feels that with Mr. Baldwin in power, a man one knows is in power. Every one feels that he is in power less because he wants to be there than because he feels the service to the State to be a moral obligation. No one has ever thought of him as a careerist, even as quite a professional politician." [8]

Assuming that nothing actually works as it appears to work is the key to understanding British political institutions, and one paradox is to be found in the Cabinet. Composed outwardly of political amateurs—laymen gathered from different walks of life and charged for the nonce with carrying on the King's business—it is really filled by professional politicians. It is true that most of them do not depend upon officeholding for their means of livelihood but, using "professional" in the sense of something a person devotes his life to, they are true professionals. And, as has been suggested, there is a long training system for Cabinet service which only the exceptional person can shorten. The prizes, as a rule, go to those who have survived the training period and possess the most seniority. In the shuffling about of seats in the National government in 1935, Sir Samuel Hoare won the Foreign Office over Captain Anthony Eden whose popularity and diplomatic successes almost overcame the good claims of his elder competitor. In the end a special place in the Cabinet, Minister for League of Nations Affairs, was found for Captain Eden. His incumbency was short, however, for a bad move made on the diplomatic checkerboard by Sir Samuel Hoare forced the Secretary's resignation and elevated his recent rival to the Foreign Office. Captain Eden remained within the charmed circle until early in 1938 when he broke with the Prime Minister's policy of further compromise with the Fascist dictators.

Captain Eden's case is a current example of the recruiting and promotions "system" for politicians in England. He is a professional politician with a typical background

[8] *Ibid.*, p. 457.

for a member of his party. By personal talent and good fortune he gained, in some fifteen years of Parliamentary experience, one of the highest cabinet posts. It is unlikely that his ministerial career is ended.

Before the War a description of political party practices would have fitted either the Conservatives or Liberals, but today qualifications must be noted for the Laborites. As mentioned previously, Labor Cabinets have been composed of professionals, veterans of many campaigns, like their Conservative rivals, but some of the Labor ministers do not wear the air of amateurishness common on the other side. It is pretty much a quality of a governing class, and an independent income is virtually essential. Some Labor politicians have been able to supplement meager Parliamentary salaries by writing and lecturing, and since these occupations are common in public life, whether done from necessity or not, they have not impaired their amateur status; but others are forced to pursue some trade or profession with a serious purpose. Many have made trade union politics a profession, and entering Parliament is simply transferring to a larger stage.[9]

It would be fortunate for England if this air of amateurishness could be retained among her politicians, for it means that service to the community rather than job-holding is made a controlling stimulus to political activity. It would be absurd to advance, of course, the proposition that all members of the governing classes have been largely motivated by this same sense of civic duty; indeed, as has

[9] Since 1906 governments have restricted more and more the business activities of ministers. They are required to resign company directorships, except those in philanthropic or personal enterprises, and the Labor Cabinet in 1924 applied this policy to trade union executives. Ministers are supposed to write for remuneration only upon historical, scientific, or literary subjects. In 1936 the resignation of Mr. J. H. Thomas was accepted when it was disclosed that some of his friends had taken out large amounts of insurance against the possibility of tax increases and that there had been a leak in the secrecy surrounding the Chancellor of the Exchequer's budget speech.—*The Times,* May 23, 1936, and June 3, 1936. See Jennings, *op. cit.,* pp. 85-88, for a discussion of the qualifications of a minister.

been suggested, many of them find the pursuit of politics a fascinating profession. However, the preservation of this tradition tends to make political life in Britain a highly respectable activity and to cause many men to act in the spirit of the tradition. When political life becomes professionalized in the sense that men enter it to find a means of livelihood or to control spoils it soon sinks low in public estimation and able men and women are deterred from entering it. In republican Germany there was some feeling that numerous Cabinet changes were made to enable politicians to qualify for ministerial pensions and, whether true or not, the belief that this selfish practice was common did not contribute to public loyalty to the Weimar regime. A great deal of American cynicism toward public life is attributable to the rather widespread conviction that the perquisites of Congressional office rather than the hope of performing a community service are the compelling influences in politicians' careers. The tenacity with which Congressmen cling to the petty nepotism of placing wives and children on the payroll as office clerks and secretaries and to the greater patronage in postmasters, relief officials, and other federal agents strengthens the conviction. In local government this type of professionalism is so taken for granted that the reasonably unselfish citizen who tries to enter politics is more under suspicion than his greedier rival.

England possesses something valuable in her tradition of amateur politicians impelled by a sense of civic duty, and it is to be hoped that the revolution in the personnel of the House of Commons during this century will not endanger this. The tradition has been part of the code of the governing classes, but it can be no less strong among the newer entrants to public life. Indeed, the Labor party since its inception has been largely dominated by men and women of strong and unselfish conviction. Mr. Baldwin has paid tribute to these people in these words: "I find in the House of Commons, especially among the

Labour Party, many men who fifty years ago would have gone into the Christian Ministry. They have been drawn into political life from a deep desire to help the people." [10] He added, "Such men are common in all parties today." If this last statement can be repeated truthfully in future years, then democratic institutions are reasonably safe in England.

[10] Stanley Baldwin, *On England* (London, 1926), p. 196.

CHAPTER IV

The Permanent Brain Trust

DURING Mr. Roosevelt's campaign for the Presidency in 1932 he attached to his entourage a number of university professors to act as advisers on the many serious economic and social problems of the day. It was not long before the smart newspaper correspondents detailed to "cover" the Democratic candidate had labelled this academic group the "brain trust." After Mr. Roosevelt's inauguration several of these professors were appointed to administrative positions, as assistant secretaries, departmental advisers, or commissioners of one kind or another. Numerous others were added to various New Deal agencies in the succeeding months.

Republican and conservative attacks upon the Administration soon singled out the brain trust for special condemnation. The most radical of Rooseveltian policies were attributed to the professors who were accused of seeking to rechristen Washington Marxville or Lenintown. The political cartoonists found the brain trust an ideal group to caricature, and across innumerable newspaper pages there dashed helter-skelter the familiar academic figure, cap and gown flying to the wind.

This episode in the utilization of professorial ability has not reacted too favorably upon the academic world. The public has assumed that all professors are impractical Utopians, bent on imposing some untried, fanciful scheme upon the country, and there has been an undeserved enhancement of the stock of the practical politician. The politicians have not been eager to discourage this sentiment in their favor. They resent the intrusion of outsiders into their realm, especially when these interlopers have received high political office—and the control of many party spoils—without having served an apprenticeship battling for votes somewhere.

The brain trust has not proved sufficiently successful to give friends of the idea that government utilize in some regular manner the research facilities of the universities an argument with which to oppose their critics. These friends can point out that many members of the Roosevelt brain trust never had much professional standing in academic circles and that their employment on administrative tasks was probably a none too happy idea. The majority of the American economists, for example, had little respect for the policies emanating from the brain trust, and meetings of these learned gentlemen were usually given over to disproving the notions of Messrs. Warren, Rogers, Tugwell, *et al.* To administrative duties many of the brain trusters brought energy and sincerity but little experience. Faced with the problem of organizing huge staffs and spending intelligently hundreds of millions within a short time, they could draw little assistance from their previous experience of directing a secretary or a few research workers within the limits of an academic budget. Some were forced to spend so much time administering that they had little left for advising on the problems to which they had devoted their study. "Professors have done too much administering, too little thinking," declares Professor W. Y. Elliott.[1]

This experience may bring Americans to a realization

[1] *The Need for Constitutional Reform* (New York, McGraw-Hill, 1935), p. 224. Professor Elliott believes, however, that the "academic field is like other professions in furnishing all types of men for this purpose, the good, the bad, and the indifferent." He points out that not all businessmen have proved themselves paragons of administrative wisdom in Washington and concludes, "Good administrators come out of the academic ranks about as often as out of other ranks."

The employment of many members of the brain trust in administrative capacities was not regarded as a successful policy by Dr. B. F. Stephens, a New Zealand municipal government authority who visited the United of the need within our national government of a reservoir of experts. Under the present system a change in the party label of the administration means a new set of officers directing the government departments. Thus the new occupant of the White House has a group of advisers hurriedly drawn together and possessed of mixed talents for their assorted duties. A new cabinet officer—and rarely have they occupied cabinet office before—finds himself dependent upon assistants as new to the job as himself. No amount of study of public problems from the outside can compensate for the lack of experience in dealing with them firsthand. Consequently, improvised brain trusts fail to be the advisory mines that they might appear to be. The permanent officials of the federal offices are all too frequently of little assistance because the methods of selecting them and the practice of reserving the important posts for party favorites usually prevent really first-class administrators from reaching high positions where they might serve as competent advisers. The departments contain many faithful employees, but they are seldom permitted by politics or training to rise above clerkships.

In the State Department a new Secretary is much more fortunate than his Cabinet colleagues, for a career service of commendable quality has developed there. He finds his Washington office and the embassies, legations, and consulates staffed with career men who have been carefully selected upon entrance. A Secretary of the Treasury has a reputable staff of expert advisers, but other Cabinet members are, on the whole, not so well blessed.

To foreign visitors the existence of such a condition in American government comes either as a confirmation of their previous opinion of the low level of politics here or as a distinct shock. After a long tour through the United States in 1935 Sir Josiah Stamp declared: "Perhaps one

States in 1936. "The professors who are the Brain Trusters at Washington should be acting as advisors instead of as administrators," he declared.— *The New York Times,* March 13, 1936.

of the essential ingredients most lacking in comprehensive American thought is appreciation of what a skilled administration means in the task of government.... There is little sense of the truth that administration is both a tradition and a technique. Some of the stories prevalent concerning the lack of prior experience of people with important tasks, which demand great administrative gifts for their success, are almost incredible." [2]

A British minister upon entering office finds a first-class corps of advisers ready at hand. They are permanent civil servants, members of the Administrative Class of the Civil Service. To them he can turn at once for counsel upon the broadest and most important aspects of his policies. In short, they compose a permanent brain trust.[3]

Almost a century ago when Civil Service reform was being cautiously considered in official circles, two doughty champions of reform, Sir Charles E. Trevelyan and Sir Stafford Northcote, pointed out that the administrative work in government departments was divisible into two parts. First, there was the routine clerical work which had to be done in every government office. Then there was the higher administrative work of advising, directing, and planning. For the first kind they advocated the recruitment of boys sufficiently schooled in the three R's to make good clerks. For the second they proposed the recruitment of some of the best products of the English universities—civil servants who would be the peers of the leading professional men of the country.

Fundamentally this is the basis of the present British Civil Service. It is composed of five general classes, subdivided into many grades, and numerous special classes,

---

[2] *The New York Times*, July 14, 1935.

[3] What is substantially the British system of departmental organization with its distinction between political ministers and non-political permanent secretaries was recommended for the American service by the President's Committee on Administrative Management. See Floyd W. Reeves and Paul T. David, "Personnel Administration in the Federal Service," *Studies on Administrative Management in the Government of the United States* (Washington, 1937), pp. 63-65.

but the principal administrative work is carried on by an army of clerks directed by this superior corps of officials. The rôle of this Administrative Class has been defined as follows: "The duties appropriate to this Class are those concerned with the formation of policy, with the coordination and improvement of Government machinery, and with the general administration and control of the Departments of the Public Service." [4]

Today there are approximately thirteen hundred officers in this class. Entrants from competitive examinations are placed in the assistant principal grade under the virtual tutorship of officers in the next higher grade. For two years they are nominally on probation.[5] After a period of from five to ten years, during which time the young officer is not merely dealing with routine matters but is given an opportunity to show his talent, he is promoted to the principal grade. As senior assistant principal or junior principal he may, if fortunate, become private secretary to the minister or the permanent secretary, thus gaining valuable experience. Later he may hope to become an assistant secretary and, if unusually capable, go on to the higher ranks, including that of permanent secretary of a department. The chief permanent officials are not restricted to the departments they enter, and it is customary to transfer them about. Most of the present permanent secretaries have served in more than one department, many of them in several. According to Sir Warren Fisher, he and his fellow permanent secretaries are constantly looking for promising officers, and when vacancies occur the whole Service is canvassed for the right men.

For many years the British have been credited with having the best civil service organization in the world, and much of this reputation has been won by the exceedingly capable Administrative Class. Americans apprised of this

[4] *Report of the Joint Committee on the Organization, etc., of the Civil Service* (1920).
[5] The best account of the training given British public officials is to be found in Professor Harvey Walker's *Training Public Employees in Great Britain* (New York, 1935).

fact wonder why the British have been able to attract to public service such an outstanding corps of officials while they have supported a mediocre service—one that periodically needs to be supplemented by a brain trust. It is rather surprising that the American service is no better in view of the fetish which Americans have made of efficiency. American business methods have been a model for the world, and from the United States have come most of the ingenious devices and mechanisms to lighten and expedite all kinds of business techniques. Yet much of the governmental work in America presents a sorry contrast to the vaunted efficiency of the great business and industrial establishments of the country. Some reasons for this situation are self-evident—an American usually sums them up with the word "politics"—but perhaps others will be suggested by a consideration of factors which have attracted young Britishers of first-class talent and education to public service.

First of all the tradition of the governing classes should be recalled. The Civil Service has always been one of the few fields into which young men of the upper classes in England could go without losing caste. Along with the military services, the Church, politics, and the professions it has received a share of the talent which these classes produced. Even young men who did not feel the spur of economic necessity or lively ambition were frequently drawn to political life of one kind or another by the paternalistic sentiment among these upper classes. Their society had a duty toward the nation to perform, and there was considerable social pressure upon young members to help shoulder the burden.

Various factors have conspired to weaken this tradition among the present-day representatives of the governing classes. Political democracy has made less distinct the line of demarcation between governors and governed, so that the former are not inclined to take their obligations as seriously. The old stigma attached to "trade" has largely disappeared, and members of old families do not hesitate to use their names and social positions to advantage in the business world. High taxation and agricultural depression have deprived many of the families in these upper classes of the economic independence which permitted them to devote time and energy to political life. They have been forced into more remunerative fields in order to maintain the scale of living to which they were accustomed. Nevertheless this tradition still has some force. The Civil Service still carries a great deal of social prestige, rising to particular heights in the Foreign Office and the Diplomatic Service, and the paternalistic tradition of the upper classes continues to draw men into government employment.

The public schools and the universities of Oxford and Cambridge have played important rôles in directing exceptional young men to the Civil Service. For generations they have been the educators of the boys and young men of these upper classes, and the traditions of these ancient institutions of learning have impressed upon the scions of the old families their responsibilities to the state. The emphasis the schools and universities place upon the classical learning has probably played its part. A young mind cannot be steeped in Plato, Aristotle, and Cicero without feeling that public life of some sort is necessary to the realization of personality.

The liaison of the universities and the Civil Service has been powerfully strengthened by the recruitment system of the latter. Since the beginning of the Civil Service reform movement it has been an axiom that the competitive examinations for appointment to the Service should be geared into the educational system of the country.[6] Examinations of increasing severity should parallel the stages at which boys and girls complete their education. Thus, the Clerical Class is recruited from among boys and girls who

[6] On the Continent this integration of the educational system and the public services is even more complete. Public education is partly the result of the need for trained personnel in government services. In England the

have completed two years of secondary school work; the Executive Class examination is designed for young men and women who have continued for two more years; and the Administrative Class examination is framed for university graduates. These competitions come annually, and the age limits are so restricted that the candidates must take the examinations soon after they leave school or the university. For clerks the age limits are 16-17 years; for executive officers, 18-19; for the Administrative Class, 22-24. Normally a young man coming down from the university will sit for the Civil Service examination a few weeks after receiving his degree. Sometimes a candidate will spend a year in "brushing up" for the examination or in travel, but unless he has received his degree at an unusually early age he will have only two or three opportunities to try for appointment to the Civil Service. This gearing together of the educational system and the Civil Service examinations has the effect of inducing many young men and women to try for positions in the public service before they seek other employment. The examinations are set as the natural culmination of a young person's education. If he has taken his university degree with honors there is a strong attraction exerted by this Civil Service examination, for it holds out the opportunity of immediate employment in a secure, honorable profession.

Besides the effort made to integrate recruitment to the Civil Service and the educational system, the type of examinations is important in attracting young, university-trained people into government service. The Administra-

---

connection does not appear to be so direct, and the desirability of educating the masses acquiring the ballot had more influence than in most Continental countries; but, nevertheless, the integration and the influence of the Civil Service upon the educational system are much more marked than in the United States. This lack of integration has intensified the problem of securing satisfactory government personnel in the United States. This point is adequately developed in C. J. Friedrich and T. Cole, *Responsible Bureaucracy* (Cambridge, Harvard University Press, 1932), pp. 24-25.

tive Class examination is designed to test young men and women not in the more or less practical work of a government department but rather in their mental equipment. There is a wide range of papers—eighty-odd—covering fields studied at the universities.[7] A candidate may choose 5 or 6 papers from this list, enough to add up to 700 points, covering a university honors course in, say, languages, mathematics, history, or natural science. To insure that all candidates have some acquaintance with the modern world in which they live, the examination includes a compulsory section covering an essay, English, and rather practical questions labeled Present Day Knowledge. This section counts a maximum of 300 points. In addition, all candidates are called for a personal interview before a board appointed by the Civil Service Commissioners, and a maximum of 300 points may be won here. The interview is not designed to test a candidate's knowledge or formal learning but his personality, taste, manners, and address. The *viva voce* examination, says Sir Roderick Meiklejohn, First Civil Service Commissioner, is like this:

There are five of us, and directly the young man comes in I try to put him at his ease, by looking at his record, and saying: "You were at Rugby; you went on from there to Corpus; you got a scholarship there." Then I should say: "What schools did you read?" He says: "Greats and Mods." I ask: "Have you any preference for history or philosophy," and he says which he has a preference for. I do not want to take all the questioning myself, so one of the others says: "Have you been abroad much?" He may say: "I have been to Germany." Then he is asked, "Did you notice any difference between Bavaria and Saxony, and the people and the customs?" The other people ask him, has he done any social work in the East End, or has he been interested in the Boy Scouts. Then we might try to find out whether he has any interest in natural history. Has he read much German or Italian literature,

[7] See Appendix I for list of subjects.

or any other language. You may ask him almost anything which occurs to you, to find out what his interests are, and how he reacts to other people and other things. It is as wide as we can make it. Of course, you ask him about his games and his sports; everything under the sun really.[8]

The marks made by the candidate on the compulsory section, the optional section, and the *viva voce* are totalled, vacancies in the Service going to the highest ranking competitors. The eligible list is used for appointments to the Home Office, the Ministry of Health, the Admiralty, and virtually all other departments. Departmental vacancies are selected by successful candidates in the order of their ranking in the examination. They are not assigned to departments on the basis of the subjects which they studied at the university.

The quality of the candidates is so good and the examination so stiff that a person with less than a university honors degree has little chance of appointment. Thus, government service claims at the start some of the keenest intellects of every generation.

A great deal has been written concerning the merits and weaknesses of the Administrative Class examination and the type of education upon which it is based. In regard to the latter, Oxford and Cambridge continue to be strongholds of the classical studies, although in recent years more attention has been paid to the natural and social sciences. The traditional schools of these universities can be defended as excellent preparation for public service in the modern state. According to Professor W. Y. Elliott:

> As a group their [the British] ruling class is trained on Plato and Aristotle at Oxford or grounded in the most abstract thought of modern science and mathematics at Cambridge. A humanistic culture, intensely philosophical and

[8] *Royal Commission on the Civil Service, 1929-31, Minutes of Evidence,* Q. 1,419.

with a rich historical perspective, is the groundwork of any long-run human development. Select the men at the top of almost any field of English life and you will find that they have had this sort of training. They have been taught to think, acquainted with the best thought, and allowed then to *grow* as minds and characters, instead of being regimented into an academic mould. The discipline is there, the games and the social tradition. But the *mind* is encouraged to find its own level by wrestling with the first minds of humanity—not in outlines or commentaries, but in the original. It does not have so many things thrust into it to digest. But it does digest some questions of permanent human interest thoroughly and well.[9]

Dr. Herman Finer, conceding that the subject matter studied at Oxford and Cambridge can be of great value to a modern administrator, believes that the tutorial method is the important asset of the old universities. "It is important to insist," he says, "that it is the method of studying and learning and not the subject of information which is of moment in selection for administration." [10] Given the study of the social sciences by this method, Doctor Finer believes "that the critical minds thus produced are of the greatest benefit to democratic government, for the politicians and the social philosophers and missionaries are only too fruitful in their proposals for reform, and the Civil Service is urgently needed as their critical assessor...."

Both the "old" and the "new" learning can be satisfactory foundations for public service. The old has demonstrated its value in the character of the ruling class of the Civil Service; the new will produce its share of capable administrators if it is studied in a liberal fashion and not allowed to degenerate into vocational techniques. The tutorial method applied to both develops powers of comprehension, discrimination, and appreciation. The student

[9] *Op. cit.*, p. 225.
[10] *The British Civil Service* (London, 1937), p. 93.

must not only absorb, but he must arrange his knowledge, evaluate it, and be prepared to defend his opinions against a skilled mind. The benefits of such study for superior students are being recognized by American universities in the introduction of honors courses.

The Civil Service Commissioners have been granting recognition to the newer studies by adding them to the examination syllabus, although the classical student is still able to assemble his 700 marks for the optional section with less effort than the student of the social sciences.

The Administrative Class examination is conspicuously open to criticism in the heavy weight it gives to the *viva voce* section. Until 1937 this part carried a weight of 300 marks in a total of 1800; now it carries 300 in a total of 1300. An interview as part of the entrance examination to the Administrative Class is desirable. The personal qualities which it can disclose are extremely important, and they are becoming increasingly so as the contacts between the public and government departments multiply. The state has a right to see that it doesn't employ what the Treasury calls "clever asses." There is little belief that the *viva voce* test is employed unfairly by the Civil Service Commissioners, although the staff side of the National Whitley Council expressed suspicions of class prejudice before the Tomlin Commission.[11] However, a statement by Mr. A. L. N. D. Houghton, Secretary of the Association of Officers of Taxes, would receive substantial agreement. He has said, "I certainly do not believe that the *viva voce* test is used as a means of 'dishing' the sons of working class parents." [12]

---

[11] Cmd. 3909 (1931), p. 69. The Commission was "satisfied that there are no grounds for any suspicion of this kind."

[12] "The Use of the Interview in Recruitment and Promotion," *Public Administration*, July, 1937, p. 323. According to Miss Dorothy Evans, "There has been no disposition to deal any way unfairly with women candidates in assigning marks, and women need not fear that their sex will handicap them before the Examining Board."—*Women and the Civil Service* (London, 1934), p. 109.

Just as may be the intentions of the interviewers, it is extremely doubtful whether they can assess the qualities they are looking for in the present *viva voce*. The number of candidates is large, the time allotted each one is short, and the questioning is haphazard. Certainly 300 marks out of 1,300 are too many for this kind of an interview. A candidate spends hours on his written examinations, amounting to 1,000 points, and yet he stands a good chance of being successful or unsuccessful as the result of a fifteen-minute appearance before a board which knows of him only through the dubious medium of tutors' recommendations. To repeat, an interview is desirable, but 100 marks would seem to be the maximum which the test should carry. A preliminary interview at the time of entry into the university, such as the Foreign Office uses, might be preferable, for then the poorest of the lot could be eliminated before they expended their efforts on the written examinations. The remainder could then be examined in a longer, more carefully prepared interview.

The effect of the recruiting system upon the character of a civil service can be observed in a comparison of the British, German, and French organizations. The British method has produced a corps of able, efficient administrators, capable of meeting statesmen, jurists, diplomats, and all other servants of the state on a plane of equality. Their education makes them cultured gentlemen, generally sympathetic and liberal in their point of view. The fact that no specialized course of pre-entrance training is required, indeed it is not desired, and the Macaulay principles of a liberal education still govern, produces an administrative corps without a caste disdain for outside professions or contempt for the other services of the state. It is a very natural branch of the general culture of British civilization.

The system has its weaknesses as well as its virtues. These weaknesses are largely the result of the fact that the recruiting system does not insure any considerable amount of contact with the many political and social problems of the modern-day world. The classical education of the young civil servant is an excellent foundation upon which to build, but he is frequently called upon to deal with very practical problems of administration before he has had an opportunity to acquaint himself with the trends of modern thought in economics, sociology, and government. There is an abrupt change from a sheltered life where he has been dealing, in the main, with theory to the decidedly vital and practical problems of a government department. Then there is a disposition on the part of civil servants to regard public administration not as a science but, as Professor Walker has said, as "an art or mystery revealed only to those who have followed the initiatory rite through which they have passed, or alternatively as a faculty inborn, which is denied to all who are not blessed with it at birth." [13] In his opinion, proper training would remedy these weaknesses.

The long, specialized training of German officials, with its emphasis upon the study of law, has produced a civil service which the term "administrative machine" aptly characterizes. It runs with remarkable smoothness and precision, but its parts belong only to an individual German officialdom. They cannot be mistaken for anything else. This bureaucracy survived the revolution of 1918 virtually intact, but felt the Nazi *Gleichschaltung* of 1933 and was purged of undesirable elements.[14] Dr. Herman Finer's comments upon the German civil service examinations and their effect bring out the contrast with the British practice. He has written:

[13] *Op. cit.*, p. 13.
[14] F. L. Schuman, *The Nazi Dictatorship* (New York, Knopf, 1935), pp. 250-52. A law of April 7, 1933, "was followed by dismissals from all branches of the public service of Jews, Communists, Socialists, liberals, pacifists, and others obnoxious" to the National Socialists. "But since the groups affected constituted only a small percentage of the bureaucracy, which the Socialists and Democrats after 1918 had left largely intact in the hands of reactionary officials, the volume of replacements was relatively small."

The striking feature of the topics set for examination is their extreme practicality and technicality, and their wide range. Not that all are technical: some are upon the history of economic and social theory. The vast majority ask for judgements upon a narrow set of circumstances; the answering of these clearly demands a fund of exact knowledge, a firm grasp of legal and economic principles, comprehension of the conditions of the effectiveness of institutions, and the ability to focus correctly the general light of science on particular cases. Little or no room is left for metaphysical adventuring, and the confines within which doubt and curiosity might arise are rather narrow. On the whole, the German procedure compared with the British shows a wide and important variation: the German being based much more upon the correct use of authorities, the British more upon personal judgements. If this diagnosis is correct the situation it reveals is important, for it may be that much of the formalism with which German bureaucracy has been charged by native critics is due to the spirit and training which have their expressions in this type of examination—nay! to the ultimate view of private and public life which engender these. The examiners believe that these are the proper questions to ask, they hold this belief because they have a mental picture of the kind of civil servant they want to secure: men learned to the point of pedantry, and logical. This produces civil servants more useful in a static than a dynamic State: excellent interpreters of the past but not inventors of the ways and means of the future: apter to explain than to evaluate; and inflexible in the power to make exceptions—which is nine-tenths of administration. Where the Germans are lacking the British are rich, but these have their own faults....[15]

The French system has certain elements in common with those of both the British and the German. For officers corresponding to the British Administrative Class or the German Higher Civil Service there is open competition but under departmental rather than general service auspices. According to Professor W. R. Sharp, "The en-

[15] *The Theory and Practice of Modern Government* (New York, Dial Press, 1932), II, 1269-70.

trance examination for the French foreign service and Council of State, in particular, is comparable in difficulty and comprehensiveness to the examinations for admission to the 'administrative class' of the British civil service." [16] However, there is considerably more legal training, after the German fashion, for the higher French officers than is the case in England, as the following account by Professor Sharp indicates:

The sort of preentrance training afforded by a university law faculty, which is the route taken by a majority of the young men contemplating life careers in public administration, combines a thorough grounding in the history and principles of French law, usually both administrative and constitutional, and in some cases civil and criminal as well, with extensive work in general economics and one or more of the following subjects: comparative government, public finance, industrial or colonial legislation, international law, and statistical method. While the inclusion of training in economics serves to counteract an otherwise narrow concentration upon law, little or no attention is given to the study of political behavior or to the technical aspects of administrative organization, personnel policy, or functional operations. The French approach to government and politics is mainly legal and philosophical, and political inquiry has always been carried on within the orthodox confines of historical and descriptive methodology.[17]

The service produced is less flexible than the British, and there is a feeling that too many of the officials have a superficial veneer of knowledge rather than real mental capacity. Favoritism has not been entirely eliminated, although it is more prevalent in promotions than in appointments, and what remains in the latter is probably less than is commonly supposed.[18]

The British have not stopped with efforts to recruit an

[16] "Public Personnel Management in France," *Civil Service Abroad* (New York, McGraw-Hill, 1935), p. 115.
[17] *Ibid.*, p. 105.
[18] Finer, *The Theory and Practice of Modern Government*, II, 1325.

THE PERMANENT BRAIN TRUST 93

able administrative corps but have also undertaken to retain it in public service. Their most obvious method has been to provide reasonable remuneration for these public servants. The scales of pay for the Administrative Class start at about £300 and rise to £3,000 for a permanent department head. The highest salaried officer in the Civil Service is the Permanent Secretary of the Treasury who receives £3,500. A recruit to the Administrative Class, of average ability, can look forward to receiving at least £1,500 during his mature years. These salaries are not large when compared to the earnings of business and professional men of like caliber, but they are adequate for comfortable living.[19] It is an elementary principle of public administration that it is necessary to provide reasonable compensation in order to retain capable men in public service and this, on the whole, the British have done. It is interesting to note that the President's Committee on Administrative Management recommended that salaries of the highest officers in the Civil Service of the United States be raised to a top range of $12,000 to $15,000.

The impression that the Civil Service loses a considerable number of officers to business and the outside professions has received some currency in recent years, and the Tomlin Commission inquired into this leakage.[20] A survey submitted to it revealed that in the previous ten years, 1920-30, one hundred and twenty-one established civil servants of the Administrative Class, in posts paying £500 or more basic annual salary, resigned from the four-

[19] See Appendix II for comparison of earnings with business and professions.

[20] In France from 1920-28 "an alarming exodus of administrative, professional, and technical personnel took place. High-grade officers were drained off to banks, industrial concerns, insurance companies, and department stores in such numbers as to jeopardize the operation of many important government services. But with the return of an interlude of prosperity (1928-32), and still more with the advent of the business depression, wholesale 'desertions' from the public service have ceased."— Sharp, *op. cit.*, p. 139.

teen large departments supplying figures to accept outside positions.[21] The largest number, forty-three, resigned to accept positions of a general commercial character; fifteen went into private practice; twelve entered the service of international organizations, quasi-public institutions, or other governments; twelve entered the academic field in connection with universities or schools; seven accepted posts with railway companies; seven transferred to local government administrations; five took "commercial posts in organizations with which the Government is closely connected"; and politics claimed two. The destination of eighteen was unknown. This number—approximately a dozen officers a year—is not as large as popular opinion would lead one to suppose it was, and in the view of Sir Russell Scott, then Controller of Establishments, the tendency to leave "is not so marked as to give cause for disquiet as to the standard of efficiency of the Civil Service." [22] There are no statistics on why these resignations occur, although Sir John Anderson, former Permanent Secretary of the Home Office, told the Commission he knew of no reason other than insufficiency of remuneration.[23] However, there are probably numerous other reasons—temperament, personal and family affairs, or a preference for active politics—as well as the opportunity for greater remuneration, and each case is an individual one. A distaste for departmental work seems to impel a good many officers to leave. Square pegs occasionally get into round holes, and after a few years of trying to grind off the edges a man may see an opening more to his liking outside the Service. What leakage occurs is more prevalent among the technical and

[21] *Royal Commission on the Civil Service, 1929-31, Minutes of Evidence,* App. XVIII, p. 1712.

[22] *Ibid.,* Q. 254. The Joint Consultative Committee, representing the upper grades of the Civil Service, informed the Royal Commission: "The number of men who actually leave the Civil Service to go into business is probably only a small proportion of those who, dissatisfied with their positions and prospects, would welcome the opportunity of doing so."— *Ibid.,* p. 729.

[23] *Ibid.,* Q. 2,254.

scientific staffs than among the administrative and clerical, and a handsome salary is usually the bait held out to these men.[24] This is not surprising, for the differences between private and public enjoyment are less marked in this field and consequently remuneration is a more deciding factor. In private employment the scientist usually receives the desirable conditions of service offered by the state—security of tenure, excellent technical equipment, and opportunities for experimentation—and, in addition, a substantially larger salary.

Probably more important than remuneration in attracting and retaining capable civil servants is the security of tenure held out. The British Service is a career service, and a young man can look forward to permanent employment if he is reasonably efficient. Legally, employment in the Civil Service is at the pleasure of the Crown, and the courts have never mitigated this rule, but actually dismissals occur only for inefficiency or conduct prejudicial to the honor of the Service.

The fact that a civil servant is a Conservative, Liberal, or Laborite makes no difference to his career. It does not figure in his appointment, and it in no way affects his advancement. In order to insulate the permanent Service as far as possible from partisan politics, civil servants are forbidden to engage in any activities connected with elections or campaigning.[25] They may vote, but they cannot make political speeches, canvass for votes, work for party organizations, contribute to campaign funds, or in any other way give public indications of their partisan sentiments. This rigorous and inflexible rule has tended to

[24] Sir Evelyn Murray, former Secretary to the Post Office, said his department had "lost some extremely good men in that way."—*Ibid.*, Q. 3,618. Data for the federal service of the United States obtained by the Personnel Classification Board indicated a similar condition in regard to turnover among the professional and scientific staffs. The separation rate was high in these services. See William E. Mosher and J. Donald Kingsley, *Public Personnel Administration* (New York, 1936), pp. 287-92.

[25] N. E. Mustoe, *The Law and Organization of the British Civil Service* (London, 1932), pp. 52-53.

make the average civil servant of the upper ranks rather indifferent to party politics. His position is secure regardless of who controls the House of Commons, and he has no stake in the continuation of any partisan regime. The contrast to American practice with its numerous politico-administrators, many of whom are retained largely as propagandists, is so obvious as to require no comment.

The career service in England has besides security of tenure other attractive features. At the age of sixty civil servants may retire on a pension, and after a few years in the Service an officer has such seniority rights and pension claims that leaving for some other employment is a serious step. The pensions system is not a contributory one, although many civil servants feel that it figures in the level of remuneration, and the government has refused to put it on that basis as many Service organizations desire and as the recent Royal Commission recommended. The present system is undoubtedly a potent influence in holding many officers to the Service when they might be inclined to leave if they could withdraw contributed pension funds. The Treasury is generous in granting pensions and gratuities to officers forced to retire because of ill health. Administrative Class officers receive annual leaves varying from six to eight weeks. While their working hours are nominally seven a day they frequently must devote many more to their duties.

Promotions within the Administrative Class are strictly on a merit basis, though, other things being equal, seniority is an important factor. They are determined by the highest-placed civil servants in the departments with the consent of the Treasury. Permanent heads of departments are selected by the Prime Minister, advised by the Head of the Civil Service who is the Permanent Secretary of the Treasury. This class is sufficiently small so that it is unlikely that an able man will fail to receive his deserts. As Sir Warren Fisher explained to the Royal Commission on the Civil Service, he and his colleagues heading departments are constantly canvassing the Administrative Class for able officers and in their zeal for an efficient Service they seldom miss a man meriting advancement.

The possession of power has long been recognized as having a great attractiveness for men of intelligence and ability, and this certainly must be mentioned as important in retaining able civil servants. Recruits to the Administrative Class early rise to positions of responsibility, and they are soon dealing with important affairs of state. As they reach the highest positions they become the confidants of ministers and the managers of vast public services. Theoretically all their acts are performed upon the order of a minister and in his name, but in the last generation the scope and burden of government have so increased that the political head of a department must leave a vast amount of real governing to the permanent officials. "Administrative discretion," Professor Laski has said, "is the essence of the modern state." [26] It is in the exercise of this discretion that the civil servants wield a vast amount of power. In addition they exert great influence over governmental policy by the direct advice they give to ministers and by the more subtle means of personality, suggestion, and criticism.[27] A prominent Englishman once remarked, "You

---

[26] Harold J. Laski, "The Growth of Administrative Discretion," *Journal of Public Administration*, April, 1923, p. 92.

[27] Lloyd George reveals in his *War Memoirs* (Boston, Little Brown, 1933-37) that the idea of the War Cabinet came from Sir Maurice Hankey, Secretary of the Committee of Imperial Defense. Lloyd George recounts their conversation during a walk in Paris. The outlook for the Allies was not encouraging. "I was in favour of immediate resignation," says Lloyd George. "To this Sir Maurice was opposed until some other means of effecting a change in the war direction had first been attempted. I can recall that as we passed the Vendome Column, Sir Maurice paused and said: 'You ought to insist on a small War Committee being set up for the day-to-day conduct of the war, with full powers. It must be independent of the Cabinet. It must keep in close touch with the P.M., but the Committee ought to be in continuous session, and the P.M., as head of the Government, could not manage that. He has a very heavy job in looking after the Cabinet and attending to Parliament and home affairs. He is a bit tired, too, after all he has gone through in the last two and a half years.

can't talk with a cabinet minister fifteen minutes on anything before he begins quoting A.B." A.B. is an important permanent official. So influential have the permanent officials become that many Englishmen are beginning to wonder who are the servants and who are the masters in their government. This question need not be explored at this point, but the statement can be made that the permanent officials possess enough power and authority to satisfy the desires of average ambition. Persons with a Napoleonic complex would find the anonymity of the Civil Service irksome, and they would be well advised to seek service elsewhere; but the ordinary human being would find sufficient exercise for this desire of the spirit.

It is true that public recognition of the civil servant's labors is rare. Except in unusual instances, "the public has little or no means of knowing how much it owes in public service to special gifts or qualities in individual civil servants in high positions in Departments of State." [28] The civil servant prepares the stage, and the minister receives the flowers—or the cabbages if there is a miscue. However, faithful and diligent service will usually merit mention in some honors list, and the winning of these tokens, relics in a democratic England of a more aristocratic past, is held in high regard by the permanent officials. Recognition in the Order of the British Empire is also open to civil servants, and the higher officers may receive the K. C. B. or other honors in the most distinguished of the orders of chivalry. For outstanding service in the foreign or colonial field there is the Most Distinguished Order of St. Michael and St. George, founded in 1818. Upon retirement a notable civil servant may be accorded some distinctive honor, not excepting a peerage.

By making the Civil Service a logical and attractive

The Chairman must be a man of unimpaired energy and great driving power...' "—II, 369-70.

[28] Earl Grey of Fallodon, *Twenty-five Years, 1892-1916* (New York, Stokes, 1925), I, xviii.

career to honors men from the universities, a career secure against the spoilsman and full of honor and prestige, the British have built up in the Administrative Class a corps of officials which has been universally acclaimed. The British themselves are very proud of their Civil Service. They have faith in its ability and its honesty. Mr. Ramsay Muir tells the story of the Tory squire, reproved by his friends for voting Labor at a general election, who explained his action by saying that the Laborites were the only politicians afraid to tamper with the civil servants.

Despite the high regard in which the Administrative Class is held there has been some feeling that perhaps the postwar recruits are not up to the standard of previous years. A suggestion of this feeling is to be found in Sir Warren Fisher's replies to questions addressed to him by the Chairman of the Royal Commission.

Q. 18,720. ... So far as you can judge, broadly speaking, are you satisfied with the type of candidate who is being recruited to the [Administrative] Class at present?—Well, some permanent Heads of Departments come to me in rather a censorious condition on the topic; others come purring, so I gather that the recruits are rather a mixed bag.

Q. 18,721. I do not know whether there is any sport in which the bag is not mixed; I do not know that one can draw any unsatisfactory conclusion from that, can one?—No.

Q. 18,722. On the whole, you do not see any reason to be pessimistic about it?—No, I think it needs watching, though. It is a subject upon which I do not feel as comfortable as I do about some things, because the importance of these men being right is not decreasing.

In reply to one of the commissioner's questions about the permanent department heads lauding the recent recruits "with harps and hymns of praise," Sir Warren Fisher stated that he believed they were exhibiting an enthusiasm in the presence of the Royal Commission which they did not entertain in less exalted moments. "I do not myself feel any doubt," he said, "that it would be putting it far too high to say that they were uniformly satisfied." [29]

Mr. A. D. Lindsay, Master of Balliol, Oxford, believed that the present entrants of the Administrative Class were hardly up to former standards. To the Royal Commission he said:

> I am judging very much on general impression. Mr. Peters [Secretary of the University of Oxford Appointments Board] has tried to get figures without very much success. I am only judging on the impression I get, year in and year out, of the most able young men, and what they go after. Also I have a general impression that men are successful now who would not have been successful before the war. It is very difficult to be dogmatic about it.[29a]

This uneasiness felt in certain quarters arises from the opinion that many of the new recruits to the Administrative Class come from social classes which in the past have had little part in staffing the public services or in shaping their traditions. The feeling has considerable grounding in fact, for the upper reaches of the Civil Service are no longer the exclusive province of higher social classes. The change has largely been brought about by the extension of educational opportunities to increasing numbers of people.

The traditional principles of making scholastic excellence the only gate to the Civil Service and integrating the educational and recruitment systems have had the effect of delivering various grades of the Service to certain social classes. This has been conspicuously true of the Administrative Class and its predecessors recruited by the old Class I examination. In prewar days its members were definitely drawn from the aristocracy, the gentry and, at the lowest, the upper ranges of the middle classes. Younger sons of

---

[29] *Royal Commission on the Civil Service, 1929-31, Minutes of Evidence,* Q. 18,914.
[29a] *Ibid.,* Q. 11,109.

good families, squeezed out of the home nest by the rule of primogeniture, had the Civil Service open to them, provided they could pass the examinations; and this type of public service carried with it as much social prestige as politics, the Church, or the military forces. The surplus which the home service could not absorb could look to India or the colonies for additional opportunities.

The monopoly which these social classes had upon the upper grades of the Civil Service was made complete by the type of examination required for appointment. An education at a university was almost essential, and the chances of success were immeasurably improved if the candidate had studied at Oxford or Cambridge. Because of the expense and centuries of tradition the students of these two great universities belonged to the upper social classes.

When open competition was a novel proposal, Gladstone foresaw that as long as the educational requirements were kept high the upper ranks of the Civil Service would remain in the hands of the traditional governing classes. He was severely abused by many ultra-conservatives for championing such an experiment in democracy, but he realized that he was granting more form than substance. And of course Gladstone was right while higher education was confined to a small part of the population.

As civil servants of an unusually high quality these men must be given their due. They made faithful and anonymous public service a challenge to some of the best of their class, and they imparted to British administration an integrity and honesty that has made it a model in the world. They avoided the arrogant, caste-like organization of the Germans and the narrow, bureaucratic tone of the French with no sacrifice of efficiency. Their abstention from partisan politics shielded them from the demoralizing place-seeking of American civil servants. They are entitled to no small share of the credit for making democracy a tolerable form of government.

It would be an exaggeration to say that the Administrative Class has been transformed and that it is no longer dominated by these representatives of the upper social ranks. As Professor W. A. Robson has said, "The Administrative Class, which occupies all the controlling positions in the Home Civil Service, consists to an overwhelming extent of the fortunate few who can manage to get to Oxford and Cambridge; and the entrance examination has always been expressly designed for that purpose."[30] But it is true that the Civil Service is feeling the impact of the new forces and trends which are reshaping much of English society. Higher standards of living, increased educational opportunities, and political democracy have not left the Civil Service untouched. The disrupting influence of the War period hastened some of these changes, but they were in the cards before the conflict quickened the tempo of the deal.

The record of the universities attended by the successful candidates for the Administrative Class, the Indian Civil Service, and the Eastern Cadetships from 1925, when open competition was resumed, to 1929 reveals that of the 414 men appointed the majority were still from Oxford and Cambridge. Oxford contributed 142 men and 3 women, and Cambridge 133 men and 2 women. Thus 66 per cent of the appointees came from these two universities. The University of London, the School of Economics and Political Science, and its other colleges, followed with 56 men and 1 woman. Excluding 21 from India and Ceylon, the report shows Dublin with 19 and Edinburgh with 17 as the next in order. The provincial universities followed with from 1 to 4 each.[31]

[30] *Op. cit.,* p. 183.
[31] *Royal Commission on the Civil Service, 1929-31, Minutes of Evidence,* p. 115. In no way facetiously it may be said that expense probably deters many candidates from Scottish universities. Besides the £8 fee for sitting for the examinations there is the expense of renting "digs" in London, and with the large number of candidates for the places to be filled many young people from over the Tweed do not care to risk a trial.

THE PERMANENT BRAIN TRUST 103

The following table shows the university distribution for the years 1930-35.[32] All successful competitors for the home Civil Service, the Indian Civil Service, the Eastern Cadetships, the Foreign Office and Diplomatic Service, the Consular Service, the Intelligence Officers of the Department of Overseas Trade, and Clerkships in the House of Commons are included. It will be noted that in 1931 Oxford lost its premier position as the educator of public servants, and the next year the number of successful candidates from that university fell to slightly less than one-fourth of the total. Oxford's loss, however, was balanced by the considerable gains of Cambridge, so that approximately three-fourths of all candidates came from the two great universities.

Oxford and Cambridge still dominate the upper ranks of the Civil Service, but even their character has changed along with most other English institutions. The general raising of educational standards and opportunities, the increased emphasis upon higher training, and especially the provision of scholarships and other aids to poorer students have opened the doors of Oxford and Cambridge to young men—and women—to whom such an education would have been impossible a few decades ago.[33] That many of them are taking advantage of these opportunities there can be no doubt.

A more accurate guide to the type of people entering the Administrative Class is supplied by the records of the schools attended before entering the universities. In former years the majority came from the famous public schools of England—Eton, Rugby, Harrow, Winchester, etc.—or their smaller and less renowned imitators. But today they

---

[32] Compiled from the Reports of the Civil Service Commissioners (1931, 1932, 1933, 1934, 1935, 1936).
[33] Three hundred state scholarships are granted each year by the Board of Education to students from grant-aided secondary schools to enable them to pursue degree courses at English and Welsh universities. Three state scholars obtained "Firsts" in "Greats" or *Literae humaniores* at Oxford in 1934.—*The Times*, August 4, 1934.

UNIVERSITY EDUCATION OF HIGHER GRADES RECRUITED BY THE CIVIL SERVICE COMMISSIONERS

Competitions for Junior Grade of the Administrative Class in the Home Civil Service and the Civil Service of Northern Ireland, for Probationer in the Indian Civil Service, for the Foreign Office and Diplomatic Service, for the Consular Service, for Intelligence Officer in the Department of Overseas Trade, and for Clerkships in the House of Commons.

University	1930		1931		1932		1933		1934		1935	
	Number	Per Cent	Number	Per Cent	Number	Per Cent	Number	Per Cent	Number	Per Cent	Number	Per Cent
Oxford	53	43.8 } 72.7	26	35.1 } 74.2	17	24.2 } 69.9	31	33.6 } 77.0	31	34.4 } 71.0	22	25.5 } 68.5
Cambridge	35	28.9	29	39.1	32	45.7	40	43.4	33	36.6	37	43.0
London	13	10.7	7	9.4	8	10.1	10	10.8	7	7.7	5	5.8
Irish Univs.	4		0		1		0		0		1	
Scottish	2		5		3		2		4		4	
Provincial & Welsh	2	} 16.6	1	} 16.4	0	} 20.0	1	} 12.2	1	} 21.1	4	} 25.5
Indian	10		6		9		6		11		13	
Foreign	2		0		0		1		1		0	
None	0		0		0		1		2		0	
Totals	121		74		70		92		90		86	

contribute a smaller proportion. Of the 408 men appointed from 1925-29, 52, or 12 per cent, attended the 9 leading public schools. The remaining 88 per cent had had their preparatory training at the smaller public schools, Indian and colonial schools, and the provided schools. Bradford Grammar School, for example, contributed as many as Eton, 6; and Nottingham High School and St. Paul's each had 4.[34]

The records of the next six years indicate the same trend, although the famous public schools make a better showing than in the previous period. The following table shows the number of successful men from the principal public schools and the number from the minor public schools and non-public schools.

The expansion of educational opportunities and the closer relationship between the minor public schools and secondary schools and the universities do not account entirely for this change in personnel in the upper grades of the Civil Service. The high rewards offered by business and the professions have had their influence, and many who might formerly have entered the Civil Service are attracted to other fields. Sir Roderick Meiklejohn, First Civil Service Commissioner, believes this is the principal reason why more boys from the famous public schools do not seek a career in government employ.[35] It has been a long time since trade and life in the commercial world were incompatible with social distinction in England, and indeed the practice has been for distinguished families to

---

[34] *Royal Commission on the Civil Service, 1929-31, Minutes of Evidence,* pp. 115-16. Mr. H. A. Roberts, Secretary of the Cambridge Appointments Board, gave an affirmative reply to Lord Tomlin's question: "Should I be right in thinking that at the present time the field of recruitment is much wider, and that a boy or girl who has been educated at a secondary school has a considerably greater chance of obtaining a post in the Administrative Class, than he would have had some twenty years ago?"—*Ibid.,* Q. 10,083. Mr. Lindsay, of Oxford, agreed that public scholarships have had an important effect upon the character of the candidates.—*Ibid.,* Q. 11,209.

[35] *Ibid.,* Q. 1,051.

recoup their fortunes in the business world. The high taxation of the postwar era perhaps has played a part in causing many young men to turn to occupations where the opportunities for large returns are greater, and the places they might have taken in the Civil Service are occupied by ambitious young people whose scale of living has not been upon so high a plane.[36]

Year	Public School		Minor Public and Non-Public School	
	Number	Per Cent	Number	Per Cent
1930	33	27.2	88	72.8
1931	16	21.6	58	78.4
1932	19	27.1	51	72.9
1933	26	28.2	66	71.8
1934	32	35.5	58	64.5
1935	19	21.8	68	78.2

A liberalizing of the promotions system has also been a factor in introducing new types of people into the highest class of the Service. In prewar days the classes of the Service were separated by virtually unsurmountable barriers but, in keeping with the more democratic idea that all ranks should be open to talented officers and because of the pressure of many organizations of employees, promotions have been more frequent and affect all classes. According to the figures given the Royal Commission by Sir Russell Scott, then Controller of Establishments in the Treasury, between 1921 and 1928, inclusive, forty-seven people were promoted to the Administrative Class while eighty-four

[36] A somewhat similar change has occurred in the recruits to the French Civil Service, and the reasons for it are much the same, although there are local factors in France to be considered.—Walter R. Sharp, *The French Civil Service: Bureaucracy in Transition* (New York, 1931), pp. 84-91.

THE PERMANENT BRAIN TRUST 107

entered by the competition route. "These figures," Professor Leonard D. White has said, "reveal a considerable breach in the traditional methods of selection from outside the service."

They are, however, considerably affected by the special provisions open to ex-service men after the war, which presumably will not be repeated in the next decade, and by the long suspension of open competition on account of post-war conditions. They are not to be taken as illustrating the type of selection which the official side thinks is desirable.[37]

While promotions in such large numbers, compared to the entrants from open competition, are unlikely in the near future, they certainly will be more frequent and numerous than in the prewar Service.[38] Consequently, the Administrative Class is going to see a small influx of officers who have risen by outstanding merit displayed in the lower classes of the Service.

The corridors of one department are still reserved almost exclusively for the representatives of the traditional governing classes, and this is the Foreign Office. Ostensibly, of course, the Foreign Office and the diplomatic service are open to all—even the old requirement of an independent income sufficient to maintain a young officer abroad for the first two years has been eliminated [39]—but the examina-

---

[37] *Whitley Councils in the British Civil Service* (Chicago, University of Chicago Press, 1933), p. 184. The promotions system of the Service was developed by a committee of the National Whitley Council in 1921. Promotions are determined largely on the basis of annual service ratings. Supervising officials rate all members of their staffs receiving less than £700 a year. In large departments promotion boards review these ratings and advise the head of the department.

[38] According to Dr. Herman Finer there were 82 officers promoted to the Administrative Class between 1923 and 1935 while 278 entered by competition.—*The British Civil Service*, pp. 107-8.

[39] In Victorian times, according to Mr. Harold Nicolson, "it was quite usual for an attaché to work without pay and on a purely voluntary basis for the first sixteen years of his service."—"The Foreign Service," *The British Civil Servant* (London, 1937), p. 50.

tion scheme for entrance places enough emphasis upon social and personal qualities to secure that very few but the public school-varsity, good-family candidate will be selected. Critics occasionally rage and fume, but so far their effect upon the placid F. O. has been unnoticeable. A few years ago a Labor member of Parliament declared in a debate on pensions for diplomats: "To enter the Diplomatic Service one must have certain qualifications. One of them is the accident of birth. One must be born in a particular stratum of society before he is admitted to the Diplomatic Service, one must have a certain kind of education and a certain income." [40]

Whereas the appeal of other government departments for the scions of the governing classes has declined somewhat, the romance of the diplomatic world and the half-mysterious air of the Foreign Office still are magnets of great attraction. To represent His Majesty the King at some exotic court or to be the guardian of great state secrets, like Sherlock Holmes's mysterious brother Mycroft, is to fill the heart's desire of most young men. So there is an ample supply of candidates, and the Foreign Office can still choose the people it likes.

Has the quality of the Administrative Class suffered as a consequence of this shift in personnel? Almost all the permanent heads of departments appearing before the Royal Commission believed that the present recruits are on a par with those of prewar days, but still the misgivings of Sir Warren Fisher and others cannot be dismissed. As a matter of fact, it is difficult to reach any definite conclusion at this time for the reason that this change has been recent and the postwar recruits are just coming into positions of responsibility. A generation or two will have to elapse before one can speak with any certainty about the result of this broadening of the area of selection.[41]

[40] *Parliamentary Debates* (5th series), vol. 222, col. 1596.
[41] Judgment will also have to be suspended for a time regarding the postwar quality of the Indian Civil Service and the Colonial Civil Service.

If a prediction may be risked, it is that this trend will cause no great change in the quality of the Administrative Class—that is, if intellectual excellence is retained as the most important criterion in selection. This opinion is based on several reasons. For one thing, while the governing classes do not find the Civil Service their exclusive province any longer, they have not abandoned it by any means. Tradition, sentiment, and desire for power still direct their steps toward it, and as administration increases in importance they will be increasingly attracted. They may discover that it is much more effective to retain control of the Administrative Class of the Civil Service as a bulwark against social revolution than Parliament. Mr. Ramsay Muir credits the Treasury officials with having turned Mr. Philip (later Viscount) Snowden "that Robespierre of Socialism into an exponent of orthodox Gladstonian finance." The administrator is succeeding to much of the power formerly wielded by ministers and legislators. So the governing classes are not likely to abandon this field without a contest, and they have brains and ability with which to fight.

Another reason lies in the fact that the great majority of the recruits still enter the Civil Service via Oxford and Cambridge, and these ancient institutions possess great power to mold and shape young personalities. They are educational establishments in the widest sense of the word,

Since the War the uncertainties of British rule in India have resulted in an insufficient supply of British candidates for the I. C. S., the staff of approximately one thousand officers who are so important in the government of that vast country. The Secretary of State for India is now authorized to select the holders of good honors degrees from universities to fill any deficiency in the quota of half-British entrants to half-Indian in the annual competitions held in London and Delhi. In 1931 a considerable amount of possible patronage was abolished in the Colonial Civil Service by substituting a competitive interview given by a Colonial Civil Service Appointments Board, chosen by the Civil Service Commissioners, for appointment by the Secretary of State on the recommendation of a private secretary. Appointments for a few colonies are made after competitive written examinations on the order of those for the I. C. S. See Finer, *The British Civil Service*, pp. 115-22.

inculcating ways of life as much as formal learning. Within their gates the traditions of the governing classes make their impression upon all indwellers. The social classes in England are reasonably fluid, and it is not too difficult for one of humble birth to ascend the scale. This is especially true for a person of ability who is assisted by residence at one of the older universities.

Entering the Civil Service the recruit is exposed to departmental traditions almost as strong as those of the universities. These demand character, integrity, and partisan neutrality of every officer. The disposition of the famous Francs Case of a few years ago illustrates how jealously the Civil Service guards its reputation. Three officials of the Foreign Office became involved in litigation resulting from gambling in foreign exchange. While an official inquiry conducted by Sir Warren Fisher, Sir Malcolm Ramsay, Comptroller and Auditor-General, and Mr. M. L. Gwyer, H. M. Procurator-General and Solicitor to the Treasury, absolved the officers of having used their official positions or any information obtained from such sources in their speculations, it declared that they acted "in a manner inconsistent with their obligations as Civil Servants." [42] For their indiscreet operations two officers were dismissed, and one was demoted.

At the conclusion of their report in the Francs Case the board of inquiry made some comments upon "the unwritten code of ethics and conduct" of the Civil Service

[42] Cmd. 3037 (1928), p. 9. The resignation of Sir Christopher Bullock as Permanent Under-Secretary in the Air Ministry was accepted in 1936 when accusations were made that he was using his official position to further private interests.

President Roosevelt was possibly seeking to avoid an American version of the Francs Case when he wrote to the Civil Service Commission as follows: "I believe it to be a sound policy of the Government that no officer or employee shall participate directly or indirectly in any transaction concerning the purchase or sale of corporate stocks or bonds or of commodities for speculative purposes, as distinguished from bona fide investment purposes."—*The Washington Herald,* April 27, 1937.

which adequately summarize its high standards and tradition.

The first duty of a Civil Servant is to give his undivided allegiance to the State at all times and on all occasions when the State has a claim upon his services. With his private activities the State is in general not concerned, so long as his conduct therein is not such as to bring discredit upon the Service of which he is a member. But to say that he is not to subordinate his duty to his private interests, nor to make use of his official position to further those interests, is to say no more than that he must behave with common honesty. The Service exacts from itself a higher standard, because it recognises that the State is entitled to demand that its servants shall not only be honest in fact, but beyond the reach of suspicion of dishonesty....

It follows that there are spheres of activity legitimately open to the ordinary citizen in which the Civil Servant can play no part, or only a limited part. He is not to indulge in political or party controversy, lest by so doing he should appear no longer the disinterested adviser of Ministers or able impartially to execute their policy. He is bound to maintain a proper reticence in discussing public affairs and more particularly those with which his own Department is concerned. And lastly, his position clearly imposes upon him restrictions in matters of commerce and business from which the ordinary citizen is free.[43]

---

[43] *Ibid.*, pp. 21-22. A high standard of official conduct developed during Germany's long experience with a professional civil service. The National Civil Service Act summarized the obligation of officials as follows: "Every civil servant is obliged to fulfil conscientiously, according to the constitution and the laws, the duties of the office conferred upon him and to prove himself in his behavior inside and outside the office worthy of the esteem which his profession requires." According to Mr. Fritz Morstein Marx, the official "code of ethics" has been upheld in practice: "First, by a potent tradition of devotion to the common weal with which the bureaucracy as a whole is permeated. Second, by the personal pride which the people takes in the efficiency, cleanliness, and resourcefulness of its governmental service. And, third, by a well-balanced and carefully judicialized system of disciplinary procedure."—"Civil Service in Germany," *Civil Service Abroad* (New York, 1935), pp. 246-47.

The new German Civil Service Act of 1937 reaffirmed the high standards

However, the most important reason for belief in the future high quality of the Administrative Class is the fact that intellectual excellence is still the only means of gaining entrance. It is still a brain trust, and there is no disposition in evidence to lower its standards. There has been some liberalizing of the examination syllabus, reducing the emphasis upon the classics and adding some of the social studies popular at London and the provincial universities. In general, though, the Civil Service Commissioners have agreed with the conclusions of a committee appointed in 1917 to consider the Class I examination.

The existing scheme [the committee said] has been condemned on the ground that it gives an excessive advantage to candidates chiefly trained in the learning of Greece and Rome. Some no doubt wish to put the classics at a disadvantage, or to exclude them altogether from the examination. We are not inclined, nor do we think it to be our duty, to put any handicap upon the widest, the most systematic, and the most consistent humanistic education that at present exists in this country.[44]

While the classical learning is under no disadvantage in the Administrative Class examination, it is falling behind as a field of study for candidates. History and modern languages are the most popular fields at present. In the 1936 competition for the home Civil Service, the Foreign Office and Diplomatic Service, and the Consular Service, the "schools" of study of the successful candidates were as follows: history, 18; modern languages, 17; history, languages, and literature, 12; economics and politics, 9; classics, 7; mathematics, 6; law, 2.[45]

---

of the Civil Service, and added that of loyalty to the Nazi regime. See James K. Pollock and Alfred V. Boerner, Jr., *The German Civil Service Act* (Chicago, 1938), pp. 10-11.
[44] Cmd. 8567 (1917).
[45] *Report of the Civil Service Commissioners* (1936), pp. 31-37.

If studied in a liberal fashion, all these subjects can be satisfactory backgrounds for public service. There certainly should be no handicap placed upon sociology, politics, and economics as fields of study for civil servants, because they can be taught, as Dr. Finer says, "to give the mind a general liberal culture as well as to give it a special cast and interest." [46] Oxford has recognized this to some degree by developing within the last ten or fifteen years the school of Modern Greats, consisting of politics, economics, and philosophy.

The principles of a liberal education and a strict standard of examinations will assure England of an Administrative Class equal in quality to the past personnel.

[46] Finer, *The Theory and Practice of Modern Government*, II, 1311.

CHAPTER V

The Administrative Army

ONE OUT OF every hundred inhabitants of Great Britain is a civil servant of the Crown. Approximately 444,000 persons are required to administer the laws of Parliament. This sizeable army is a very diversified one, for there is scarcely a trade or profession that is not represented. So diverse have become the types of people who staff the government departments that they comprise a cross section of British society at its widest extent.

A stroll to the entrance of one of the great Whitehall offices will easily demonstrate this fact. Suppose we make our visit in the late afternoon when the offices are emptying for the day. There in the doorway is the porter, a grizzled old Briton with a museum exhibit of medals on his coat. With a little prompting he could be induced to relate campaign tales stretching from "India's sunny clime" to muddy days at Arras when the Boche transferred him to civil employment. A flash of the old days returns as he straightens to attention and murmurs, "Good day, my lord," to a dignified gentleman coming up the steps. "Aye, the Secretary of State," he informs us. The question hour in the House of Commons over, he has hurried back to his office to give a hasty but practiced glance at a few important papers and consult with his general manager, the permanent secretary, and then he must dress for that livery company dinner in the City tonight.

But while the Secretary's business day is far from closed, his office staff is on its way home. Here come dozens of chattering young girls, the flappers of the penny papers.

Hands and arms tired from typing or operating a tabulating machine, their thoughts are transferred to Southend or perhaps the latest picture at the Stoll. Here come crowds of uniformly dressed men—young, middle-aged, and some close to the retirement mark—clerks hurrying to the tube or bus stations. This monotony of dark suits, bowler hats, and umbrellas is relieved occasionally by a feminine counterpart who is exercising her right to a more colorful costume. What office does that sternfaced woman in the tailored clothes occupy? No doubt she is a pensions or works inspector for the Home Office, and the short man is telling her that she should be glad she's relieved from prying into places like that hot brewery which was on his route today. These next two must be professors. Not quite —they are chemists who are still discussing a technical problem which they have gone over with the assistant secretary into whose province falls the traffic in dangerous drugs. A newly advanced principal, who still retains a little of his undergraduate youthfulness, salutes our friend the porter with his stick. A week-end in the country would be nice, he thinks, but not much chance with three pardon appeals hanging fire. And then into the corridor moves a squad of creeping charwomen to prepare the offices for a new day.

There still remain many other kinds of civil servants, and visits to the arsenals, the dockyards, the engineering laboratories of the Post Office, labor exchanges, and scores of governmental institutions would be necessary to cover all categories. These thousands of employees may be catalogued as follows: [1]

1. Clerical, Executive, and Administrative Officers.. 60,300
2. Professional, Scientific, and Technical Staffs, Inspectorates, etc. 24,900
3. Writing Assistants, Temporary Clerks, and "P." Class Clerks 30,300
4. Typists and Shorthand-Typists 8,500

[1] Figures for 1931. The "P." Class has since become the "S." Class.

5. Manipulative Staffs (Post Office sorters, postmen, etc.) 181,800
6. Messengers, Porters, Charwomen, etc. 17,200
7. Industrial workers (dockyard and arsenal workmen, Post Office linesmen, etc.) 121,400

Total 444,400

These civil servants are employed in some 85 departments. The largest is the Post Office in which the staff totals approximately 228,240 employees.

With the transformation of the laissez-faire state of the nineteenth century into the positive state of today there was a consequent increase in administration and the size of the Civil Service. Coincident with an increase in size came greater specialization. The bifurcation of the Service which had occurred in 1870 when open competition for most positions was adopted was still recognized in principle, but by 1914 the introduction of numerous new classes and grades had split the Service below the First Division (now the Administrative Class) into complex hierarchies, usually different for each department. The clerk was still the typical civil servant, but he had become surrounded on all sides by specialized groups of employees. Above him had been inserted the Intermediate Class to perform more responsible kinds of work. Below him were new classes to perform routine functions such as filing, recording, and typing. On every side there were specialists, technical officers, inspectors, and manipulative employees doing work of a nonclerical nature. Some simplification in the organization of the Service was badly needed to promote efficiency and to prevent injustice to the employees arising from different conditions of service. Such a reorganization was proposed by the able MacDonnell Commission which investigated the Civil Service just before the War. It suggested the integration of numerous departmental classes of employees into a small number of all-Service classes having common scales of pay and working conditions. However, the MacDonnell Commission had the misfortune to report just when the European concert was breaking up into a dozen military bands, and its recommendations had to be laid aside until a more propitious time to consider domestic matters should arise.

The World War was such a tremendous upheaval of society that it is customary for the present generation to regard it as the end of one era and the beginning of another. Perhaps historians a few centuries later will draw the boundaries between epochs somewhere else, for today we can do little more than hope that the cynics who write of the *first* World War are wrong. At any rate, those living in the first half of the twentieth century find the postwar world sufficiently different to justify the opinion that those grievous days marked some kind of a turning point.

The British Civil Service obviously could not pass through such a period unchanged. The War sucked from its ranks thousands of men for military service, and at a time when the state required additional employees in large numbers. Ninety per cent of the Assistant Clerk Class, for example, saw military service before the end of the conflict.[2] Temporary employees were recruited to fill the vacant ranks, and at the peak as many as 60,000 were serving.[3] Women were employed in increasing numbers, so as to release men for military service. Ten new departments, such as the Ministry of Munitions and the Ministry of Pensions, were created, more than 160 boards and commissions were established, and old departments were expanded far beyond peacetime requirements. Previous methods of recruitment to the Civil Service had to be suspended or revised because of the absence of former sources or the inability of the government to use the care formerly exercised. The loss of relationship with prewar standards of value necessitated new methods of remunera-

[2] *Royal Commission on the Civil Service, 1929-31, Minutes of Evidence,* App. II, p. 15.
[3] *Ibid.*

tion, and the induction of thousands of new types of employees into the Service and the tumultuous conditions of War days resulted in labor troubles that required quick rather than altogether satisfactory settlements. Concession and compromise were frequent, for the necessity of winning the War surpassed all other considerations. Hence, the Civil Service which emerged from the War period was considerably different from the one which entered those stormy years.

The government perceived the confusion likely to ensue at the close of hostilities, and therefore undertook to evolve some policies for returning the administrative machine to a peacetime basis. Almost a year before the Armistice the Treasury created a commission under the chairmanship of Lord Gladstone to propose methods of appointment until open competition could be resumed, to consider the employment of discharged service men, to study the future status of the large temporary staffs, and to suggest policies which would establish within a few years a service on the lines contemplated in the MacDonnell report. The Gladstone Committee urged a reclassification of the Civil Service, recommending the regrouping proposed by the minority report of the MacDonnell Commission.[4]

This important matter was taken in hand by a committee of the National Whitley Council, which had been formed in 1919 after the government had decided to apply to its staffs the report of the Ministry of Reconstruction Committee on the relations between employers and their workers. This Reorganization Committee was "to consider the scope of the duties at present allotted to the Clerical Classes in the Civil Service; to report on the organization most appropriate to secure the effective performance of these duties; and to make recommendations as to scales of salary and method of recruitment." After stating that

[4] "Report of the Gladstone Committee," *Parliamentary Papers* (1919), XI, 12-14.

an "effective division of labour is of the very essence of sound administration," the Reorganization Committee proposed the creation of a hierarchy of five general classes in the Civil Service: an Administrative Class, an Executive Class, a Clerical Class, a Writing Assistant Class, and a Typist Class.

During the year 1920 the assimilation of the existing general and departmental classes to the new scheme of organization was begun. The First Division became the Administrative Class; the Second Division became, with the Intermediate Class, the Executive Class, to the extent to which the new class could include them; the Assistant Clerks became the Clerical Class; and the small Writing Assistant Class, existing only in the Post Office and the Ministry of Health, was absorbed in the new class of the same name. Women Clerks became members of the Executive or Clerical Classes. This assimilation was departed from somewhat in 1921 by the creation of departmental Clerical Classes in several offices, and so today there exists a dual form of organization. The common hierarchy of classes is the one outlined by the Reorganization Committee, although not all classes are found in every department; but in some offices departmental clerks on lower rates of pay are employed.

Thus, it was not until after the World War that a considerable degree of unity was brought into the Civil Service by the creation of general classes, running through the majority of the departments, on common scales of pay. There had been a few common classes previously, the First and Second Division Clerks for example, but departmental autonomy had prevented any large-scale assimilation in an all-Service scheme. The postwar reorganization was to some extent marred by the creation or the retention of some departmental classes in the clerical sphere. The staff organizations declare that this was because of the desire of the government to economize at the expense of its employees; the official position is that these departmental classes are engaged on work sufficiently dissimilar from the general classes to justify their existence. In 1936 both sides presented their arguments before the Industrial Court in a case instigated by the Civil Service Clerical Association, which was determined to get some action on this controversial issue. Taking a cue from across the Channel, the Association even considered a stay-in strike. The award of the Court gave higher pay to several thousand departmental class clerks, and thus the staff contention was in effect accepted as the more meritorious. The Civil Service Clerical Association "has won probably the greatest victory yet achieved in the Industrial Court," stated a Service journal in a leading article.[5] Continuing, the editor declared, "What the Court has done has been deliberately to reject a recommendation of the Tomlin Commission. . . ."

Despite the fact that a unified Civil Service organization was not achieved until fairly recently, a considerable amount of unity was established long ago through what is known as Treasury control. A definition of Treasury control is not simple. An attempt by Mr. Henry Higgs, a former principal clerk of that department, may serve better than an elaborate analysis. "Treasury control," Mr. Higgs has said, "is something you live under, that you suffer from, that you profit by; and if you cannot define it, well—Lord Morley used to say that he could not define an elephant, but he knew it when he saw it, and you know Treasury control when you feel it."[6]

For a very long time the estimates of a department have had to pass the scrutiny of the Chancellor of the Exchequer, but only in the last few decades have detailed staff matters been supervised by the Treasury. As the entire administrative machine has become more highly unified through common examinations for appointment, the creation of general classes, and the institution of uni-

---

[5] *Civil Service Opinion,* November 15, 1936.
[6] "Treasury Control," *Journal of Public Administration,* April, 1924, p. 122.

versal service regulations, the need for a supervising agency has grown, and Treasury control, because of the peculiar constitutional position of that department, has been the answer to that requirement.[7] Treasury control in respect to staff matters was further enhanced by the creation in 1919 of an Establishments Department within the Treasury as an organ of supervision, and by the bestowal upon the Permanent Secretary of the Treasury of the additional title, "Head of the Civil Service." Treasury control was made complete by an Order in Council of July 22, 1920, which empowered the Treasury "to make regulations for controlling the conduct of His Majesty's civil establishments, and providing for the classification, remuneration and other conditions of service of all persons employed therein, whether permanently or temporarily."

Within the department the minister is still responsible to Parliament for the correct conduct of his office, and Treasury control stops short of interfering with or derogating from the minister's responsibility. Appointments to departments are made in his name, promotions—at least within classes—are determined by him, and disciplinary cases are departmental matters. However, all important decisions on staff questions are in the province of the Treasury. Just as the House of Commons established its supremacy through the power of the purse, so the Treasury by means of its check over departmental finance has become paramount in staff matters.

[7] Just what legal sanction Treasury control possesses seems buried in constitutional history. Mr. Higgs has written, "The theory upon which all that [Treasury control] rests is that the Letters Patent which constitute the Board of Treasury put into commission the Royal Prerogative as far as financial matters are concerned, and therefore when the Treasury says, 'You must take this off your budget, or you cannot do this, that or the other,' it is really speaking in the name of the King whose money it is, and therefore it is the supreme constitutional authority upon the question."—*Ibid.*, p. 126. Sir Henry Bunbury has suggested that "Treasury control may depend on Section 27 of Exchequer and Audit Department Acts, 1866."—"Financial Control Within Government Departments," *Journal of Public Administration*, April, 1924.

As the result of a policy advocated by Sir Warren Fisher, the Permanent Secretary of the Treasury, the permanent secretary in each department is also the accounting officer, responsible for financial regularity in the expenditure of appropriations and for economy in the management of his department. He reports to the Public Accounts Committee of the House of Commons upon questions of financial regularity, and he and his fellow permanent heads "work together as a team in the pursuit of economy in every branch and every detail of the public service." [8] Each department head is assisted in matters of staff management by an establishments officer, who is in constant contact with the central personnel office, the Establishments Department of the Treasury. The Controller of Establishments effectively manages all important personnel matters through a standing committee of these departmental establishments officers and the individual officers.[9]

The lower ranks of the Civil Service have not been especially happy as this growth of Treasury power has proceeded. Mr. W. J. Brown, General Secretary of the Civil Service Clerical Association, told the Royal Commission that "we think that the fact that the central coordinating authority is the Treasury ... emphasizes to an undue point financial considerations at the expense of other considerations." [10] Despite this and numerous other criticisms of Treasury control, the Royal Commission felt that the weight of opinion was in favor of the present arrangement. Its conclusion was, "We recommend no changes in the present system." [11] It found no merit in the idea, advocated

---

[8] *Royal Commission on the Civil Service, 1929-31, Minutes of Evidence,* p. 1273.

[9] An account of the growth of Treasury control in recent years may be found in Don K. Price, "Administrative Co-ordination in Great Britain and the United States," *Public Administration,* October, 1935, pp. 377-84.

[10] *Royal Commission on the Civil Service, 1929-31, Minutes of Evidence,* Q. 6,020.

[11] Cmd. 3909 (1931), p. 171.

by some staff groups, of a personnel department independent of the Treasury.

Accompanying better organization in the Civil Service has come an improvement in the administrative personnel. Nearly all witnesses before the Royal Commission on the Civil Service agreed that the quality of the entrants to the Executive and Clerical Classes was good and that after training many of them were worthy of promotion. The personnel of the Executive Class compares favorably with the former Second Division Clerks, who were probably superior to people doing somewhat analogous work outside the Civil Service. For the Writing Assistants (now known as Clerical Assistants) and Typing Classes there has been no difficulty in recruiting satisfactory staffs of young women. At a recent competition for Writing Assistants, 75 per cent of the successful candidates had been educated at secondary or private schools, and only 8 per cent came from elementary schools.[12] The ability of the girls selected has been slightly above the caliber of the work they have had to perform, and many eligible for the Clerical Class competition have entered the lower grade in the hope of promotion.

The expansion of educational opportunities for the masses has largely been responsible for the improvement in administrative personnel. Public education has given the state a wider and wider circle from which to draw its servants. The boys and girls thus educated, and also their parents, look upon the Civil Service as a choice field of employment. Considering the security of tenure offered, pension rights, and other conditions of service, they regard its scales of remuneration as attractive. In addition, employment by the state carries enough prestige to be in itself a considerable inducement to young people leaving school. The public generally is acquainted with the fact that the entrance examinations are hard and the number of competitors is large, so all successful candidates are re-

[12] *Ibid.*, p. 16.

garded as fortunate boys and girls. The father of a working class family feels that his child has a good start in life if the latter wins a job in the Civil Service.[13]

Considerable credit for improving the quality of Civil Service employees of all grades must be accorded the Civil Service Commission, the body created in 1855 to examine entrants to public departments. Its competent personnel has maintained high standards for entrance, and with an enlarging area of recruitment it has offered to the departments well-qualified people for appointment. The caliber of the Commission's examinations has reacted upon the educational system, because authorities must maintain good schools in order to offer their pupils a chance at Civil Service positions.

The postwar quality of the Civil Service personnel seems to have suffered in only two conspicuous instances, and they are the cases of the temporary clerical staff and the "P." and "P.U." classes. They are almost entirely a War legacy. Of 30,350 "P." and "P.U." class clerks, temporary clerks, temporary shorthand typists, or temporary typists employed in 1931, 98.7 per cent entered after April 1, 1914, and 91.1 per cent after April 1, 1918.[14] A great proportion of them are ex-service men substituted for temporary employees taken on during the War years. Competitions for positions in the established service following recommendations of committees under the Earl of Lytton and Lord Southborough enabled the best of these employees to be absorbed into the regular classes, but thousands who either failed in the examinations, did not take them, or were employed later remained on a nominally temporary footing. About 8,000 ex-service men were granted permanent but nonpensionable employment by the Guinness Agreement of 1925, constituting the "P."

[13] In 1936 there were 6,246 candidates in the General and Departmental Clerical Class Examination. Fifteen hundred were successful, 1,014 boys and 486 girls. In 1935 there were 3,830 candidates. Thus there was a 63 percent increase in candidates in 1936 over the previous year.
[14] Cmd. 3909 (1931), p. 151.

and "P.U." class. Concerning these employees the Royal Commission stated:

> The calibre of the existing "P." and "P.U." class and temporary clerks varies considerably. There is, however, no doubt that in general their standard of efficiency is lower than that of members of the clerical classes recruited by open competition. A considerable proportion of the "P." and "P.U." class and temporary clerks are employed upon writing assistant duties and are not suitable for employment upon better duties.[15]

Since of more than 12,000 of these employees in departments other than the Ministry of Labor, where the labor exchanges create a peculiar condition, about 70 per cent had served at least ten years and about 85 per cent at least five years, the Royal Commission recommended that they be given established status in an obsolescent class to which no further appointments would be made after August 1, 1934. This grant of permanent status was to include all temporary clerks serving continuously since April 1, 1926, and all who should complete five years' continuous service on or before August 1, 1934.

This recommendation of the Royal Commission was considered by a committee composed of official and staff representatives in 1932, and as a result establishment was granted to the "P." and "P.U." class, temporary clerks, and temporary typists who had served since April 1, 1926, and whose employment had been reasonably continuous. The "P." and "P.U." class and the temporary graded men clerks were placed in a Special Class, from which officers may be promoted to the general or departmental clerical classes.[16] Thus this postwar problem, which has been complicated by the fact that the state undertook to employ as

[15] *Ibid.*, pp. 153-54.
[16] *Report of Temporary Staffs Committee* (1932). Temporary employees of the Ministry of Labor were treated the same as those in other departments. This department had 14,312 unestablished employees in 1931.—Cmd. 3909 (1931), p. 162.

many ex-service men as possible, is in a fair way toward solution.[17] It will not be cleared up entirely until the "S." class disappears with the lapse of time, and for the present the Service must suffer this class below its ordinary standards.

The necessity of caring for these large blocs of ex-service men also had the effect of delaying the resumption of open competition, and this closed the opportunity for Civil Service employment to many boys and young men maturing after the War. The loss of new blood from the schools extending over a period of several years probably will appear more strikingly in the future as the older men of the present Service pass out and their places are filled from below.

With the passage of the free and easy era of patronage and a constant improvement in the personnel of the lower ranks of the Civil Service there has come considerable self-assertiveness on the part of the staff. In the old days Mr. Gregory Hardlines, of Trollope's satire, *The Three Clerks,* could rule his office as a petty autocrat, restrained only by his superiors. His clerks were usually devoid of ambition and quite content to sit at the same desk year in and year out, as long as a fairly decent salary was received, or until fortune should smile from an unexpected quarter. Appointed through favor or luck, they had no particular claim upon further consideration, and as they frequently had pitifully little education or ability they were constrained from pressing for privileges or advancement which might raise embarrassing questions. When death or retirement created a vacancy it might be filled by a new recruit who had an influential patron, or the senior man below might move up. Theirs was not to ques-

---

[17] The state has given employment to a large number of ex-service men. Of 311,874 civil servants employed on April 1, 1934 (industrial staffs excluded), 49.7 per cent, or 155,160 employees, were ex-service men. Disabled men comprised 14.9 per cent of the total nonindustrial staffs of the departments.—Cmd. 4621 (1934).

tion the division of labor in offices, the salaries paid, the promotions made, or the discipline meted out.

However, this humility waned with the professionalization of the Service. The recruits who had won positions through the competitive examination system were not content to have their future careers controlled by the capriciousness of superior officers, and abetted by the general spread of democracy in British institutions they have demanded and won a right to be heard on questions affecting their conditions of employment. In order to increase the pressure of their views they have resorted to organization on the lines of labor in outside industry. The first Civil Service unions appeared in the Post Office in the latter part of the nineteenth century, and today there are several hundred covering all grades and classes. Approximately four-fifths of the some 350,000 nonindustrial civil servants belong to unions.

Civil Service trade unionism received a great boost in 1919 when the government adopted the Whitley council system for its employees, for it is only through an association of his class or grade that an officer can be represented in this plan. Discussion, consultation, and agreement between the government on the one hand and organized employees on the other form the essence of the system. Both because of the Whitley system, which has given the associations regular and important machinery to exercise, and the growth in size of many associations, the professional union official has become a common figure in the Civil Service. Many of the larger unions maintain salaried secretaries to represent them in negotiations with the Treasury and to carry on Whitley council business.

The development of unionism has not been looked upon too favorably in official quarters, for there has lurked the fear that a highly organized Service might feel strong enough to use its power to coerce the state in some important issue. The close relationship between the Civil Service organizations and outside trade unionism did nothing to allay these apprehensions. Behind the Trade Union Congress was the Labor party, dependent upon the T.U.C. for most of its leadership and sinews of political warfare.

The issues inherent in Civil Service unionism were brought dramatically to the fore in the General Strike of 1926. Had a majority of the Civil Service unions made common cause with their outside brethren the state would have stood virtually shorn of its right arm in its determination to break this resort to coercion. The Civil Service associations did not join the striking unions, but a majority of them clearly revealed where their sympathies were. Anticipating that during this crisis civil servants might be called upon to perform additional and special duties, the staff side of the National Whitley Council advised all associations to restrict their members to only normal functions. This attitude precipitated a schism in the ranks of the Civil Service, and the Joint Consultative Committee, representing officers in the higher classes, withdrew from the National Whitley Council.

The attitude of a large proportion of the Civil Service during the General Strike caused the government to attempt to insure that in a future crisis of this nature it would not be struck down from behind. It did this in Clause V of the Trade Disputes and Trade Unions Act, 1927. Briefly, this clause forbade the membership of civil servants in any but Treasury-approved unions, and required that they be strictly Service organizations, unaffiliated with outside unions or political parties. "The bill was received very quietly in the civil service. Executives protested, the editors of service papers denounced it in leaders, association secretaries fulminated in speeches; but it aroused no violent resentment among the general body of civil servants, or even of association members." [18] Probably several reasons account for this passive attitude. One certainly was

[18] J. H. Macrae-Gibson, "The British Civil Service and the Trade Unions Act of 1927," *The American Political Science Review,* November, 1929.

THE ADMINISTRATIVE ARMY 129

that among many civil servants and even some important associations there had been considerable dissatisfaction with the political purposes of the unions and their obvious connection with one party, and these employees and organizations welcomed the divorce which the act required. This undoubtedly was the sentiment of the officers in the higher grades. Others were perhaps cowed by the failure of the strike: they were scarcely in a protesting mood. Whatever reasons caused civil servants to accept the act with little protest, they were sufficient to induce co-operation with the government in establishing the new order. No association failed to apply for a certificate of approval, and the Treasury rejected none. Only a considerable *esprit de corps* could have accomplished this after the tense days in 1926 and the bitter contest over the bill in Parliament.[19]

While relying principally upon their associations to present their views on Service questions, civil servants have not overlooked the opportunity of electing members to the House of Commons to represent their interests directly. "Dockyards members" have been familiar figures for years, but only recently have the nonindustrial staffs

[19] A bill similar to the Trade Disputes Act was proposed in France in 1920, but the organized employees defeated it and ignored a subsequent decree dissolving the *Fédération des Syndicats de Fonctionnaires*. Ministries have "vacillated from a sort of *de facto* recognition of employee *syndicats* to renewed attempts to outlaw their existence...."—Walter R. Sharp, "Public Personnel Management in France," *Civil Service Abroad*, p. 142.

Civil service trade unionism never became a serious problem in Germany. "The Deutscher Beamtenbund during republican days stood for the principle that 'the common welfare has to take precedence over private interests of the public servant,'" and it refused to champion the right to strike. Under the Hitler regime unionism in the Civil Service "was welded into one single mass organization, the Reichsbund der Deutschen Beamten, which in its top structure was connected with the National Socialist Party headquarters."—Marx, *op. cit.*, pp. 257, 269.

For the attitude of the German courts on the right to strike, see F. F. Blachly and Miriam E. Oatman, "German Public Officers and the Right to Strike," *The American Political Science Review*, February, 1928, pp. 157-61.

sought to place spokesmen on the green benches. The liaison of the Civil Service associations and the outside trade unions produced a natural interest in the Labor party among thousands of the state's employees, and in the general election of 1924 two representatives of Post Office organizations won seats as Laborites. If the Conservative party hoped to nip this development in the bud as one of the results of the Trade Disputes Act—and it certainly had this in mind—it was to be disillusioned; for in 1929 seven Civil Service spokesmen, mostly paid secretaries of larger unions, were returned to the House of Commons.

However, in some staff circles this policy is looked upon as not worth the candle. Electing a member is expensive business—one association is said to have expended £10,000 getting its secretary into the House of Commons—and his influence is not proportionate to the outlay. If he is on the government side he probably will be sitting far from the Treasury bench, and his influence will be proportionately remote; if he is with the Opposition, he cannot be of much service to the interests which backed his election. He can ask questions to call attention to some grievance, but then that can usually be arranged without direct representation. The House of Commons is disposed to leave most matters affecting administration to the ministry and the Treasury, so there is little opportunity for a Civil Service representative to promote staff matters. When Labor was in power with Snowden as Chancellor of the Exchequer the practice of a nonpolitical Civil Service was as carefully observed as previously. If attempts are made in the future to elect Civil Service representatives, many staff leaders favor the policy practiced by the teachers of getting members in all parties. This insures them representation however the election goes, and it will tend to eliminate a partisan flavor from their demands. It is very questionable whether even this policy would pay commensurate dividends.

In the Whitley council system the civil servants have

found a more satisfactory means of dealing with their employer than in the election of members to Parliament. Under this system representatives of staff associations meet in departmental and all-Service councils with their immediate employers, members of the Administrative Class, to consider virtually all questions affecting conditions of employment—remuneration, promotions, leave, pensions, etc. Decisions reached by the councils, and both sides must agree, are effective unless the government of the day disapproves.

Like most innovations, Whitleyism in the Civil Service has neither fulfilled the high hopes of many of its advocates nor the dour predictions of prophets of woe.[20] The departmental councils have been more successful than the National Council, probably because, as Sir Russell Scott has stated, the discussions "are so much more in the family and more domestic, and are mainly conducted by people who are actually familiar with the work that is being done." [21] The National Council has been pretty much a diet of words. According to Sir Warren Fisher, "it seems to have become more or less a debating society, rather academic and sometimes a little oratorical, which no doubt is very good in its way, but does not have much relation to practical business." [22] Some staff representatives criticized the Council before the Royal Commission in a similar vein. Mr. C. A. W. Sanders, an officer in the Customs and Excise Department, where a departmental coun-

---

[20] For a brief appraisal of the Whitley system, see F. G. Birkett, "Whitleyism in the Central Government Service," *Public Administration*, April, 1936, pp. 169-80. See Appendix III for the composition of the Staff Side of the National Whitley Council.

[21] *Royal Commission on the Civil Service, 1929-31, Minutes of Evidence*, Q. 622. One departmental council, however, broke down completely for a time. This was in the Post Office where official recognition of a secession from a union produced an impasse which led to the suspension of the council. It has been restored, but the necessity of dealing with the secessionists through an Extra-Whitley Committee still prevents its smooth functioning.

[22] *Ibid.*, Q. 18,752.

cil has operated very successfully, cited the practice of members of the national body rising to speak as being symptomatic of its unsatisfactory and laborious procedure. To the Commission he said:

> It has led to long speeches. It is an effort to continue speaking sitting down, and one does not go on speaking unless one has something to say; but when one stands up it is different, and it attracts a certain type to the staff side. We get a tendency to get orators instead of business men, and on the other side we have a number of Heads of Departments who are not accustomed to stand up to speak and who lose the thread of discussion.[23]

Some of these heads of departments have not been very co-operative on or off their feet. "Whitleyism," Professor White has said, "has not succeeded in inducing official initiative, proposing matters to the staff for joint consideration. The staff have not been met halfway...." [24] Where it has been successful there has occurred the happy combination of able staff representatives and a sympathetic, co-operative official side.

The National Council has some creditable achievements to its record nevertheless. The reorganization of the Civil Service in 1920, the fluctuating bonus system of remuneration, improvements in the promotions machinery, and several other important changes in the Service were introduced or made via the Whitley path. Yet Civil Service Whitleyism has progressed little beyond the realm of bread and butter issues. It has been absorbed almost exclusively with economic matters, and the trade union atmosphere has dominated its councils. The hopes of many that Civil Service Whitleyism might be the means of discovering and utilizing valuable techniques in public administration have not been realized, but perhaps they may be when the important economic problems of the postwar era fade

[23] *Ibid.*, Q. 7,753.
[24] Leonard D. White, *Whitley Councils in the British Civil Service*, p. 349.

from the scene. What little has been done of a noneconomic character is a seed which will have to be carefully nourished if it is not to be starved in discussions over wages, leaves, hours, and equal pay. "At worst the councils will probably remain important negotiating bodies for economic differences; at best they may become the means for expressing the inventive and creative power of the service." [25]

In addition to the Whitley councils civil servants have conciliation and arbitration open to them as a form of negotiation with their employer, the state. Introduced during the World War when soaring prices made wage adjustments necessary, arbitration was abolished in 1922, the government declaring that Whitleyism made it superfluous. However, the staff associations campaigned vigorously for its renewal, and in 1925 the government yielded. The Civil Service was brought within the provisions of the Industrial Courts Act of 1919. The staff groups have sought a separate arbitral tribunal, and in 1936 this was achieved.

The Civil Service Arbitration Tribunal is composed normally of the president of the Industrial Court and two members selected by him from panels drawn up by the Minister of Labor to represent the staff side of the National Whitley Council and the Chancellor of the Exchequer respectively. Its jurisdiction covers claims affecting the emoluments, weekly hours of work and leave of classes of civil servants, and resort to the Tribunal is open to government departments, recognized staff associations, and the National and departmental Whitley councils. No individual claims are considered, and classes receiving in excess of £700 a year are excluded. Since the reintroduction of arbitration in 1925 approximately twenty-five cases a year have been heard, and they have consisted principally of demands for some revision of wages or hours, favorable to the staff, based on alleged discriminations suffered by

[25] *Ibid.*, p. 350.

the complaining class when compared with other employees. Subject to the overriding authority of Parliament the government has agreed to give effect to the awards of the Court.

It is rather difficult to determine the principles upon which the Court makes some of its awards. Sometimes it seems to follow a tit-for-tat policy, allowing the Treasury to win a case and then a staff association; or it may grant only a part of a claim, thus giving some satisfaction to both sides. Without doubt the financial condition of the country enters into the Court's awards, for it was less generous during the dark days of the economic depression. It should be remembered, however, that this is an arbitration body and not a court of law, and it cannot be judged by the same strict standards. In one thing it can be compared with an ordinary court, and that is in respect to its conduct. On this point the Court deserves a high rating. In the hearing of the cases the Court is scrupulously fair, and neither side feels that it was not permitted to do itself justice.

In general it may be said that while agreeing to compulsory arbitration the government has confined it to as narrow limits as possible. By interpreting the terms of reference to the Court and by excluding all matters not falling expressly under the questions which may be arbitrated, it has not allowed its control over the Civil Service to be greatly weakened by this machinery. Unless the principle of almost complete self-government for the Service is granted, it is impossible for the government to commit itself to an extension of arbitration. Arbitration is more than a means of approach and negotiation, and as long as governments are held responsible for the conduct of public departments and must perform state functions with an eye to the financial burdens imposed they cannot surrender final authority in staff matters.

CHAPTER VI

The Civil Service and the Public

IN THE days after the World War, whenever many Britishers were particularly appalled at the rising costs of government, or were distressed by the encroachment of the state in one field after another, or were confronted with an apparently inexplicable governmental decision, they found a ready scapegoat in the word "bureaucracy." The bureaucracy was responsible for heavy taxation, it designed new activities for the state to assume, it snooped on honest citizens, and it was constantly plotting against the country's best interests. The bureaucrat, whose humble, innocent mien concealed the master schemer that he was, was cast in this sinister rôle by many of his countrymen. In the chase after the bureaucratic fox newspaper editors frequently led the pack and encouraged the yelping of others who joined in once the pitch was set.

The *Morning Post,* in a repentant mood, reminded its readers in a leading article in 1932 of the current attitude toward the Civil Service.

In our current state of national tribulation, we are a little apt to curse the Civil Service, and die. The taxpayer finds it a relief to blame the Inquisition as he scratches his head over his Income Tax form. The man of business, revolving in the night-watches the law of diminishing returns, exclaims that the Civil Service is eating up the country. The soldier and sailor, harassed by perpetual demands for economy, find it difficult to repress the retort—"What about the millions wasted in Whitehall?" The Press makes caricatures of effete old gentlemen spending their time in slumber while the country goes to ruin. The people, who think, with justice, that their fathers were happier and more prosperous without all these departmental regulations, point to the vast increase in the cost of the administration, and contrast the unhappy lot of those who must feel the full force of the blizzard with the sheltered state of the salaried and afterwards pensioned official. All this criticism feeds a grudge natural enough in the circumstances....[1]

Much of this criticism of bureaucracy came as a reaction to the general state of affairs in postwar England. It was usually not very specific in its accusations, except upon the subject of departmental costs, and it struck out blindly at a convenient target—convenient because a tradition of neutrality and anonymity forbade any rejoinder by civil servants. They might supply politicians with counterblasts, but the latter frequently did not desire to reorient the battle although believing in the general innocence of the sufferers.

In addition to the general attack upon bureaucracy, the Civil Service has fallen afoul of two more specialized groups of critics. These new critics have not been as numerous as the general objectors to bureaucracy, but they have been more pointed in their attacks and usually they have been firing from superior positions. There has been a good deal of armament borrowing among these warriors, and the battle fronts have not been kept clearly delineated. One of the new forces charged the Civil Service with an invasion of the rights and liberties of British subjects. Books, such as Lord Chief Justice Hewart's *The New Despotism,* Sir John Marriott's *The Crisis of English Liberty,* and Mr. C. K. Allen's *Bureaucracy Triumphant,* accused the administrative officials of a lawlessness which endangered the ancient liberties of Englishmen. Another group of critics found the upper ranks of the Civil Service lacking in a proper appreciation of and a satisfactory attitude toward the grave social and economic problems confronting modern Britain.[2]

[1] October 24, 1932.
[2] Criticisms of the organization of the Civil Service, conditions of service, etc., are being ignored here since they are largely internal problems and only indirectly affect its relations with the public.

This last opinion has been mentioned above in connection with the Administrative Class of the Civil Service. Briefly, the burden of the complaint is that the highest officers of the Civil Service are prevented by social station, education, and environment from appreciating the needs of the day, and that they unconsciously—for almost never is their good faith questioned—commit sabotage upon progressive policies in the name of economy, efficiency, or practicability. The "inarticulate major premise" from which they argue needs revision. Naturally most of this type of criticism emanates from Labor party circles, and more from the intelligentsia than the practical politicians.

The importance of a "right" attitude among high-placed civil servants does not need to be stressed. Their growing influence in the political process makes it imperative that they be open-minded and progressive and not rigid adherents of any particular social or political philosophy. By an obscurantist attitude they could do a great deal to set the brakes upon policy which they consider objectionable.

However, certain conditions prevent this possibility from being as real as it might seem to be. Traditions of neutrality, reinforced by security of tenure, predispose civil servants to play the game according to the rules their political chiefs declare, although they do not hesitate to present their opinions before decisions are made with all the force they can muster. One permanent secretary confided that he literally had to shout his views to a headstrong minister, but after their tumultuous conferences he loyally executed the orders of his superior. Also, while many of these civil servants do not have educational backgrounds designed along the most modern lines, they have broad cultural educations which are conducive in intelligent officers to open-mindedness and tolerance. A revision in the number of marks assigned to subjects in the Administrative Class examination syllabus, so as to weight more heavily the social science disciplines, would go far toward satisfying the critics who complain on this score. This change, they feel, would tend to produce a better balance among the types of people recruited for this class.

The attack upon the Civil Service for its disregard of certain traditional liberties has been much more formidable—so much so that an official investigation and report have been necessary to appease the critics. Briefly, the charge is that civil servants, abetted by grasping ministers and careless members of Parliament, have encouraged the wholesale delegation of legislative and judicial power to government departments. This power, critics say, has been exercised by civil servants in an arbitrary and highhanded manner.

The Committee on Ministers' Powers, under the chairmanship of the Earl of Donoughmore, K.P. (Sir Leslie Scott, K.C., later succeeded him), was appointed by Lord Chancellor Sankey on October 30, 1929, and it submitted its report in 1932. The Committee was composed of members of both houses of Parliament, civil servants, and representatives of the academic world. It was appointed "to consider the powers exercised by or under the direction of (or by persons or bodies appointed specially by) Ministers of the Crown by way of (a) delegated legislation and (b) judicial or quasi-judicial decision, and to report what safeguards are desirable or necessary to secure the constitutional principles of the sovereignty of Parliament and the supremacy of the Law." [3]

The Committee took notice of the principal criticisms levied against delegated legislation. It summarized them as follows:

(1) Acts of Parliament may be passed only in skeleton form and contain only the barest general principles. Other matters of principle, transcending procedure and the details of administration, matters which closely affect the rights and prop-

[3] Cmd. 4060 (1932), p. 1.

erty of the subject, may be left to be worked out in the Departments, with the result that laws are promulgated which have not been made by, and get little supervision from Parliament. Some of the critics suggest that this practice has so far passed all reasonable limits, as to have assumed the character of a serious invasion of the sphere of Parliament by the Executive. The extent of its adoption is, they argue, excessive, and leads not only to widespread suspicion and distrust of the machinery of Government, but actually endangers our civic and personal liberties.

(2) The facilities afforded to Parliament to scrutinize and control the exercise of powers delegated to Ministers are inadequate. There is a danger that the servant may be transformed into the master.

(3) Delegated powers may be so wide as to deprive the citizen of protection by the Courts against action by the Executive which is harsh, or unreasonable.

(4) The delegated power may be so loosely defined that the area it is intended to cover cannot be clearly known, and it is said that uncertainty of this kind is unfair to those affected.

(5) While provision is usually made
    (a) for reasonable public notice, and
    (b) for consultation in advance with the interests affected, where they are organized,
this is not always practicable, particularly where the public affected is general and not special and organized.

(6) The privileged position of the Crown as against the subject in legal proceedings places the latter at a definite disadvantage in obtaining redress in the Courts for illegal actions, committed under the authority of delegated legislation.[4]

While recognizing the importance of these criticisms the Committee on Ministers' Powers found that "they do not destroy the case for delegated legislation." [5] In fact, the Committee was of the wholly natural opinion that the practice of delegating a considerable amount of legislative power to the executive was advantageous in the modern state. "But in truth," the Committee said, "whether good

[4] *Ibid.*, pp. 53-54.
[5] *Ibid.*, p. 54.

or bad the development of the practice is inevitable. It is a natural reflection, in the sphere of constitutional law, of changes in political, social and economic ideas, and of changes in the circumstances of our lives which have resulted from scientific discoveries." [6]

The problem, then, was one of safeguards, and to this the Committee addressed itself. It took the criticisms of delegated legislation to indicate "that there are dangers in the practice; that it is liable to abuse; and that safeguards are required." [7] It was not disposed to be greatly alarmed over the present state of affairs, for it felt that the admitted defects of the methods and procedures connected with delegated legislation were "the inevitable consequence of its haphazard evolution," [8] and that they might be eliminated by certain changes of practice and law. The excellent study of delegated legislation in England made by Mr. John Willis confirms the Committee's opinion that delegated legislation has had a long haphazard evolution and is not a postwar plot of the bureaucracy.[9] "A long period of imperceptible growth, a quickening to meet the felt needs of the new Social State, a sudden flowering during the War, and after the War the full fruition—such is the history of delegation in England, not difficult to trace out after the event, but, except for a voice here and there, crying in the wilderness, disregarded in its making by lawyer and statesman alike." [10]

The Committee on Ministers' Powers proposed some fifteen recommendations to eliminate abuses and establish safeguards in connection with delegated legislation. In

[6] *Ibid.*, p. 5.
[7] *Ibid.*, p. 54.
[8] *Ibid.*
[9] *The Parliamentary Power of English Government Departments* (Cambridge, Mass., Harvard University Press, 1933).
[10] *Ibid.*, p. 5. From the middle of the nineteenth century onward acts containing delegations of power become fairly common. "Henceforward [from *c.* 1850] instances of delegation become progressively more frequent until in 1919 sixty out of the one hundred and two Acts passed delegated legislative power."—p. 20.

Recommendation I the Committee suggested a simplification of nomenclature in order to eliminate the chaos of verbiage resulting from the indiscriminate use of "regulation," "rule," and "order." Recommendation II stated: "The precise limits of the law-making power which Parliament intends to confer on a Minister should always be expressly defined in clear language by the statute which confers it; when discretion is conferred its limits should be defined with equal clearness." [11] In England a proper functional distribution of governmental power has been deemed desirable, but in the absence of a dogmatic assertion of the principle in a written constitution there has been a generous delegation of legislative power to the executive. In the United States, where the principle of the separation of powers is embedded in the fundamental law, there has developed of necessity the widespread practice of conferring subordinate legislative and judicial power upon the President and administrative officers and bodies. The limits of this delegation were unknown until the Supreme Court in 1935 called a halt. In the "Hot Oil" cases [12] and later in the famous Schechter case [13] the Court declared there had been an unconstitutional delegation of legislative power to the executive branch of the government, and the justices demanded substantially what the Committee on Ministers' Powers was recommending to Parliament, namely, that there be "precise limits" to the lawmaking power granted. Probably the American courts will always be more exacting than the conscience of Parliament in regard to the necessity of precise limits, standards of guidance, and clear statements of policy where delegation is involved, but it is interesting to note that the English committee is asking for somewhat the same thing the Supreme Court declares the Constitution of the United States makes mandatory.

[11] Cmd. 4060 (1932), p. 65.
[12] *Panama Refining Company* v. *Ryan, Amazon Petroleum Corporation* v. *Ryan*, 293 U. S. 388 (1935).
[13] *Schechter* v. *United States*, 295 U. S. 495 (1935).

Recommendations III and IV concern that interesting legislative device nicknamed the "Henry VIII clause." Such clauses permit a minister actually to modify the provisions of an Act of Parliament. The Committee recommends that such a far-reaching power should be "abandoned in all but the most exceptional cases." [14] This will not entail any great sacrifice since the clause has been used much more sparingly than it is commonly supposed.[15]

Next, the Committee recommends that clauses excluding the jurisdiction of the courts should be "abandoned in all but the most exceptional cases." [16] Recommendation VI proposes that in such exceptional cases the statute should set forth the intention of Parliament in plain language, and the following recommendation is that in all other cases "there should not be anything in the language of the statute even to suggest a doubt as to the right and duty of the Courts of Law to decide in any particular case whether the Minister has acted within the limits of his power." [17]

Recommendations VIII and IX propose amendments to the Rules Publication Act, 1893, and its general applicability. The necessity of some regularized procedure for giving publicity to administrative orders is plain. The strictures which the United States Supreme Court in the Hot Oil cases passed upon the uncharted maze of orders and rules issued by the federal government indicate the need of some similar reform in Washington.[18] Here the

[14] Cmd. 4060 (1932), p. 65.
[15] Willis, *op. cit.*, pp. 164 ff.
[16] Cmd. 4060 (1932), p. 65.
[17] *Ibid.*
[18] *Panama Refining Company* v. *Ryan*, 293 U. S. 388. *The Federal Register*, appearing for the first time March 14, 1936, may supply this need. Published daily except Sundays and Mondays, it is devoted to executive orders and proclamations, rules and regulations of general interest issued by government departments. The necessity of some order in the American system is discussed by Ervin N. Griswold, "Government in Ignorance of the Laws—a Plea for Better Publication of Executive Legislation," 48 *Harvard Law Review*, pp. 190-213.

Supreme Court discovered that a lower federal court had decided a case upon NRA code provisions which had been amended previously without either the court or the parties concerned knowing of the change.

Recommendations X and XI advise the extension of the departmental practices of consulting interests especially affected by administrative legislation and appending explanations to new regulations or rules.

The next three recommendations concern safeguards recommended to insure adequate scrutiny of rules and orders by Parliament. The Committee recommended that there be adopted a standardized procedure for laying regulations, except when an affirmative resolution is required by an act, before Parliament for possible annulment. The Standing Orders of both Houses should require that every bill conferring lawmaking power presented by a minister "should be accompanied by a Memorandum drawing attention to the power, explaining why it is needed and how it would be exercised if it were conferred, and stating what safeguards there would be against its abuse." [19] Then the Committee recommended the creation in each house of Parliament of a small standing committee to scrutinize and report on proposed delegations of legislative power and regulations and rules laid before Parliament. The Committee recognized that the absence of some automatic machinery for the scrutiny of both proposed cases of delegation and rules made under existing statutes was a serious fault in the present procedure for guarding against abuses, and it came to the conclusion that committees would have to do what had been everybody's business and consequently had usually been nobody's business.

Finally, Recommendation XV emphasized the importance of able drafting—"an art requiring specialised knowledge"—in the preparation of regulations and rules.[20]

[19] Cmd. 4060 (1932), p. 67.
[20] F. F. Blachly and Miriam E. Oatman propose a central rule drafting bureau for the government of the United States to produce some standard-

Disposing thus of delegated legislation, the Committee on Ministers' Powers turned to the subject of judicial and quasi-judicial decisions by ministers. It rejected Professor Robson's proposal for the establishment of a system of administrative courts and administrative law, believing that "they are inconsistent with the sovereignty of Parliament and the supremacy of the Law." [21] It felt that there was "nothing radically wrong about the existing practice of Parliament in permitting the exercise of judicial and quasi-judicial powers by Ministers and of judicial power by Ministerial Tribunals, but that the practice is capable of abuse, that dangers are incidental to it if not guarded against, and that certain safeguards are essential if the rule of law and the liberty of the subject are to be maintained." [22] A brief summary of the Committee's recommendations will indicate the safeguards thought necessary.

Recommendation I stated: "Judicial, as distinct from quasi-judicial, functions should normally be entrusted to

ization of form and guarantee of legality.—*Administrative Legislation and Adjudication* (Washington, 1934), pp. 89-90.

[21] Some proposals of the American Bar Association's Special Committee on Administrative Law are interesting in this connection. This committee recommended:

"In principle and with certain exceptions, the judicial functions of federal administrative tribunals should be divorced from their legislative and executive functions, and should be placed:

"(a) preferably in a federal administrative court with appropriate branches and divisions including an appellate division, or, failing that

"(b) in an appropriate number of independent tribunals (or a combination of such tribunals and an administrative court) analogous to the Court of Claims, the Court of Customs and Patent Appeals, and the Board of Tax Appeals,

"in either case the tribunal to be limited to judicial functions, its members to hold office during good behavior or at least for long terms of years, the tribunal to have power to make use of commissioners or examiners and to establish branches and hold hearings anywhere in the United States, and its decisions to be subject to judicial review to the full extent permitted by the Constitution. In the future, no judicial power should be delegated by Congress to any non-judicial tribunal other than in accordance with the foregoing."—"Report of the Special Committee on Administrative Law," *Advance Program of American Bar Association* (1934), pp. 200-1.

[22] Cmd. 4060 (1932), p. 115.

the ordinary Courts of Law, and their assignment by Parliament to a Minister or Ministerial Tribunal should be regarded as exceptional and requiring justification in each case." [23] Secondly, the Committee declared that in any exceptional cases a ministerial tribunal rather than a single minister was preferable. By Recommendation III the Committee proposed to leave quasi-judicial decisions with individual ministers unless some departmental interest was liable to interfere with his impartial attitude as a judge. Throughout its consideration of these problems the Committee emphasized the necessity of a judicial attitude and recognition of the principles of "natural justice" on the part of administrators. Only in a properly recruited and organized civil service can the judicial attitude survive. Overzealous, partisan, improperly trained administrators cannot be judicious. Recommendations IV, V, and VI pertain to the conduct of administrative cases, and recommend opportunities for affected parties to state their cases, reasoned decisions by ministers, and the publication of reports of statutory public inquiries which precede judicial or quasi-judicial decisions by ministers. Recommendations VII, VIII, IX, and X refer to the right of the subject to appeal to the courts from ministerial decisions. The Committee believed that the "jurisdiction of the High Court of Justice to compel Ministers and Ministerial Tribunals to keep within their powers to 'hear and determine according to law,'... should be vigilantly maintained," and that an aggrieved party should have an absolute right to appeal on any question of law, although, as a general rule, there should be no appeal on a question of fact.[24] The legal procedure for such appeals should be simple and expeditious, in the Committee's opinion.

The Committee confessed that under the rule of law "the remedy of the subject against the Executive Government is less complete than the remedy of subject against

[23] *Ibid.*, p. 116.
[24] *Ibid.*, p. 117.

subject." [25] However, it believed that a measure on the lines of the Crown Proceedings Bill, submitted in 1927 by a committee presided over by Sir Gordon (now Lord) Hewart, "would fill the lacuna." [26]

The report of the Committee on Ministers' Powers gave little comfort to the critics of administrative law and justice. In so far as they were complaining about the exercise of legislative and judicial functions by the executive, the report indicates that their cause is lost. The "inevitability" of this development is admitted throughout. These critics must complain to Parliament for passing statutes so broad or upon such technical subjects that the lawmakers cannot foresee specific applications or comprehend highly intricate details. Since the interference of government in the complex social and economic life of this day is so taken for granted, there does not appear to be any possibility of these critics inducing Parliament to revert to simpler forms of legislation. "The truth is that if Parliament were not willing to delegate lawmaking power, Parliament would be unable to pass the kind and quality of legislation which modern public opinion requires," declared the Committee on Ministers' Powers.[27] For the critics of the "lawless" manner in which executive and administrative officials have exercised the powers conferred upon them, the Committee offered the safeguards outlined above. If given effect, the Committee believed that the supremacy of Parliament and the law would remain real.

The Committee absolved the Civil Service, so frequently the target of the shafts hurled by the critics of "bureaucratic tyranny," from any blame in either the development of administrative law and justice or their improper use.[28] In regard to the Henry VIII clause, the acme of executive

[25] *Ibid.*, p. 112.
[26] *Ibid.*
[27] *Ibid.*, p. 23.
[28] It is interesting to note, however, that Lord Thring as Parliamentary Counsel believed in delegating details and procedural matters, and his successors have continued to encourage the practice.—*Ibid.*, p. 24.

usurpation, the Committee said, "We dispose, in passing, of the suggestion, unsupported as it is by the smallest shred of evidence, that the existence of such provisions in certain Acts of Parliament is due directly or indirectly to any attempt or desire on the part of members of the permanent Civil Service to secure for themselves or for their Departments an arbitrary power." [29] In regard to all phases of this subject of administrative law and justice the Committee assured the public that it saw "nothing to justify any lowering of the country's high opinion of its Civil Service or any reflection on its sense of justice...." [30]

Despite the clean bill of health which the Committee on Ministers' Powers gave the Civil Service, it suffered some loss of prestige during these years when it was the subject of frequent attacks. How far it dropped in public esteem cannot be measured, but from random statements it seems to have been less highly regarded in many quarters than before the World War. A few years ago a newspaper correspondent could write, "A long course of attacks in the Press and in the House of Commons (where the ephemeral politician is always a little jealous of the Permanent Official) has set a curious and unworthy impression of the Civil Servant on the public mind—he is commonly viewed as a rapacious, but slothful animal that sleeps for long periods in a pigeon-hole lined cosily with red tape." [31] This is an exaggerated picture, and most critics emphasize the grasping or the pedantic qualities of civil servants rather than their indolence. A half century ago this indolence was the butt of many jokes, such as the old quip which likened the civil servants to the fountains in Trafalgar Square, playing from ten to four. But whatever line the present-day critics have taken, their barbs are symptomatic of the public attitude.

The loss of prestige which the Civil Service has suffered

[29] *Ibid.*, p. 59.
[30] *Ibid.*, p. 7.
[31] *The Morning Post*, October 24, 1932.

has probably diverted some possible candidates to business or the outside professions. In times past the high prestige value of Civil Service employment compensated in large part for the comparatively low salaries paid to important officers; but with that impaired by a barrage of criticism, what remains is not always sufficient to attract a proper share of the best talent leaving the universities. This diversion has not reached serious proportions, but many high ranking officers are anxious about the future. They are particularly fearful that with the passing of the business depression and the appearance of more opportunities in the commercial world the attractiveness of the Civil Service will decline still further in comparison.

The public attitude toward the Civil Service has not affected recruitment for the lower ranks as far as can be discovered. The social classes from which these officials come have not been critical of the postwar bureaucracy as the wealthier and better-educated classes have been, so it has suffered little diminution of prestige in their eyes. They eagerly compete for positions in the Service, and they regard success in gaining employment as a lucky turn of the wheel of chance.

In spite of attacks made upon Whitehall the general public in Great Britain has a considerable measure of respect for its Civil Service. Among all classes there is confidence in its integrity and disinterestedness. Professional and business men, on the whole, have genuine respect for the ability of the principal civil servants. A prominent barrister who had known many ministers and civil servants once remarked that he always felt that the permanent officials had a little edge on their political superiors in mental equipment, and such a view is shared by numerous other people. Generous delegations of power to the administrative departments have been palatable in Great Britain in large part because of the public's faith in the neutrality and integrity of the Civil Service. Much of the objection to delegation in the United States is probably an unconscious appreciation of the frequently low caliber and partisan character of administrative officers, and the general confidence in the federal judiciary has permitted it to interfere in the legislative process to a degree that would not be tolerated if its personnel did not enjoy such a high reputation. Many British critics have begun to see that their fire was misdirected and that the Civil Service has not deserved the charges brought against it. Advocates of a socialized state are realizing that to destroy the high repute of the Civil Service will seriously impair the most vital machinery of their new order, and Conservatives are discovering in it a valuable balance wheel to violent swings of policy. As evidence of this turn in sentiment a Conservative newspaper has declared:

> The public, ... for its own advantage, would do well to stop sneering at the Civil Service. If its repute vanishes finally, Whitehall may turn into a nest of clever asses and meddling, busy bureaucrats. A nation, it is said, gets the Government it deserves; but heaven help us if we get the Civil Service we have been trying to deserve.[32]

The Civil Service has been anxious that the public think well of it. The Service has guarded its honor and integrity jealously, and swift retribution has fallen upon any officer who has "let it down." The disposition of the Francs Case indicates how careful the Service is that the public feel absolutely confident that civil servants are thoroughly honest and loyal to their trust. The Service has been considerably disturbed over "the constant stream of innuendo against it, sometimes broadening out into open attack."[33] Sir Warren Fisher, Permanent Secretary of the Treasury, stoutly defended the Service against any of these criticisms in his evidence to the Tomlin Commission. He rebutted, by figures on the military service of its members, the charge that during the War the Civil

---

[32] *The Morning Post,* November 5, 1932.
[33] *Royal Commission on the Civil Service, 1929-31, Minutes of Evidence,* Statement of Sir Warren Fisher, p. 1269.

Service constituted one huge "funk hole" swarming with "Cuthberts," and denied the accusation that it is "really engaged in a bureaucratic conspiracy for its own aggrandisement, against the liberties of the rest of the community." [34] In another connection Sir Warren indicated his desire that the Service be kept in high repute with the public. Commenting upon the remuneration of the highest officers, those receiving £3,000 a year, he said.

> I would under no circumstances, even if you had a bulging Exchequer and a most prosperous country, recommend any alteration of that rate. My reason is not that it has any relativity to what such men would command in comparable positions outside (for these are general managers of very large and difficult businesses), but again for the reason that you would have an easy, cheap attack started up, which would be damaging to the Service.... [35]

Some resentment may develop within the Civil Service at the comparatively high salaries paid managing directors of some of the public corporations; e.g., the London Passenger Transport Board. Salaries two or three times those of permanent department heads are not uncommon. The status of the employees of a number of these bodies vis à vis the Civil Service raises some interesting problems for the future. Salaries twice as great as those received by permanent department heads in the Civil Service are paid to many local government officers.

The desire of the Service to maintain a favorable public opinion is exemplified in the care taken to insure that people receive prompt and courteous treatment from government offices. It was not always so. Sir G. W. Kekewich has described the attitude at the Board of Education in years gone by toward correspondence.

> If a man had the temerity to write to the Office [he said], we felt he ought to take his chance of an answer.... We con-

[34] *Ibid.*
[35] *Ibid.*, Q. 18,743.

CIVIL SERVICE AND THE PUBLIC 151

sidered an early reply would be an inducement to him to continue the correspondence—a result which was naturally regarded by us as undesirable.... In the rooms of the Secretary and the Assistant Secretary might be seen many piles of papers strapped together, waiting for a sudden access of energy on the part of the official responsible for their despatch.[36]

Today the chronic letter writer and the crank get the same courteous treatment that is accorded the person seriously seeking information or registering a legitimate complaint. Even the officials of the Post Office, who come in contact with the public more than any other servants of the Crown, give very satisfactory service, sometimes under considerable provocation. A few years ago the Bridgeman Committee on the Post Office declared:

From the evidence we have heard and from personal observation we believe that the vague generalizations as to inefficiency and discourtesy on the part of the subordinate staff are exaggerated. Instances do undoubtedly occur, but we believe that the staff as a whole are genuinely anxious to give their best service to the public, and we see no reason to believe that they compare unfavorably so far as efficiency is concerned with any other body of employees of similar magnitude.[37]

A word should be said about the red tape which so frequently exasperates the private citizen when he deals with a government office. Delays, letter writing, filling in forms, investigations, seeking approval of superiors, these are some of the incidents of government work which often seem meaningless to the public. During the War there appeared in England an amusing satire called *Jonas Rowbottom and the Cow-cake*. Farmer Rowbottom, trying to

[36] Quoted in *The Morning Post,* October 24, 1932.
[37] Cmd. 4149 (1932), p. 42. In an effort to give the Post Office a better "press," a Public Relations Officer was appointed. "Almost coincidentally attacks in the press were discontinued, Post Office affairs came to have a news value, laudatory leading articles began to appear; indeed it almost seemed that the Post Office could do no wrong."—Birkett, *op. cit.,* p. 176. The Civil Service Confederation has a publicity officer to reply to unfair press attacks.

get some feed for his cow, became enmeshed in governmental regulations, and it finally took a royal commission to rescue him. Alas, the cow was dead by then. Government service frequently breeds petty bureaucrats to whom routine, no matter how useless, becomes sacred. The public is justly critical of these officials. On the other hand, a great deal of the red tape which seems wasted, unnecessary effort to the private citizen is forced upon officials by the nature of public service. They are acting usually in the name of a chief who is responsible to Parliament and the public, and there must be records which he can call for upon occasion. No one knows but that some insignificant administrative act—the purchase of some supplies, the demolition of a building, the refund of a tax payment—may be the basis for a public inquiry, and records reaching back for years may be demanded. Many officials are probably involved in one administrative action, and the most feasible way to keep them all informed is through memoranda. Officials are tending to confer in person or by telephone more often, but the necessity for records of the steps taken limits the use of these contacts. Unlike most private businesses, government offices are under an obligation to treat all citizens with the same consideration, and a routine procedure is the best way to insure this. "Thus red tape correctly used is the symbol of the citizens' equality before the law." [38]

One method of assisting in the development of a favorable attitude among important interests and of insuring a good reception for administrative regulations has not been exploited as completely as it might be, and that is the use of advisory committees. The practice of establishing advisory committees of professional or interested parties was used before the War in such instances as the Board of Education Act, 1899, the Trade Boards Act, 1909, and the National Insurance Act, 1911, and it was greatly ex-

[38] K. B. Smellie, *op. cit.*, p. 422.

CIVIL SERVICE AND THE PUBLIC 153

tended during the War years.[39] Since 1918 their use has grown in favor. In practically all recent inquiries into public administration the advisory committee idea has won approval. The Machinery of Government Committee declared that to retain public confidence departments must "avail themselves of the advice and assistance of advisory bodies so constituted as to make available the knowledge and experience of all sections of the community affected by the activities of the Department." [40] Again the Committee said:

So long as advisory bodies are not permitted to impair the full responsibility of Ministers to Parliament, we think that the more they are regarded as an integral part of the normal organisation of a Department, the more will Ministers be enabled to command the confidence of Parliament and the public in their administration of the services which seem likely in an increasing degree to affect the lives of large sections of the community.[41]

Professor Laski, who has set forth the desiderata for constituting such committees, concludes that "of the value of advisory bodies, there is now no room for doubt." However, he finds that where they exist at ministerial discretion the outstanding fact concerning them "is their wraithlike character. They are merely concessions to a sense that they are means of securing public confidence in the work of a department; but there is no evidence that they are in any way substantial."[42] There are limits, of course, to the profitable employment of such bodies, but it seems clear that these have not been reached.

[39] John A. Fairlie, "Advisory Committees in British Administration," *American Political Science Review*, November, 1926.
[40] Cmd. 9230 (1918), p. 11.
[41] *Ibid.*, p. 12.
[42] *A Grammar of Politics* (London, 1925), p. 376. Friedrich and Cole point out that "advisory committees have existed on the continent of Europe for centuries, for example in commerce; the French *Conseil National Economique* is an outgrowth of such an advisory committee, established under Henry IV."—*Op. cit.*, p. 5.

In conclusion, then, the Civil Service seems to have been attacked in the postwar years more harshly than it deserves. The critics who rail at the bureaucracy for the increasing cost of government and the extension of governmental functions should direct their weapons at the politicians who make campaign promises or who hold theories of public functions which extend the province of the state. Indeed, the virtue which the Treasury makes of economy and this department's control over the entire administrative machine make the British Civil Service less guilty of self-stimulated growth than is the service of almost any other country. The remarkable fecundity of *Messieurs les Ronds-du-Cuir* is taken for granted by the public in every country, but in England more of the responsibility rests with Parliament than with the Civil Service.

As for the criticism that the principal civil servants are not alive to the problems of their day, there is some measure of truth in this. As a body they seem to entertain moderate views on current problems; certainly their ranks contain few aggressive social reformers, and also few reactionaries. Probably their views represent a fairly accurate cross section of intelligent British opinion. A slight tendency toward conservatism or traditionalism is probably attributable to their social and educational backgrounds, and this draws criticism from quarters which are eager to be pushing ahead more rapidly. There is danger that they will not supply enough of the "thinking" that modern government requires. While this is primarily the job of the ministers and members of Parliament, it must also be shared by those whose experience with the actual operations of government gives them a foundation from which they can propose, plan, and invent with skill and accuracy. Civil servants of the Sir Robert Morant type are always necessary. Statesmen-administrators they might be called. Sensitive to public need and expert enough to surmount the administrative problems involved, they can assist ministers in making a permanent contribution to the nation's welfare.

That the Civil Service is engaged in a plot to rob Englishmen of their hard won liberties, or even that they are callous toward the rights of private subjects, is fanciful; but, as the Committee on Ministers' Powers pointed out frequently in its report, present administrative procedures are liable to abuse and should be corrected. That this can be done was the Committee's firm conviction. While no great tyranny can be alleged, hundreds of petty injustices can mount into a great wrong, and with the state becoming an increasingly important factor in every citizen's life it is imperative that its procedures be modernized. When industrial machinery was simple, simple protective devices sufficed, but high-speed modern machinery requires more elaborate protection for the operative and the mechanic. So with government. A century ago it moved slowly and with obvious strides; today it moves rapidly and the whole mechanism is so large no citizen can comprehend it all. Hence, improved protective methods must be adopted to prevent that precious heritage, liberty, from being crushed in the wheels. Some believe that this can only be done through the adoption of a supplementary judicial system on the model of Continental countries; others believe the traditional English system will suffice.[43] A fair trial of the latter reformed along the lines of the recommendations of the Committee on Ministers' Powers would seem to be in order.

[43] According to Friedrich and Cole, "The modern legalized government can be made responsible to the courts for the acts of every member of its organization. It is a minor problem whether this function is exercised by the regular courts or by specialized 'administrative' courts; and the solution of the problem depends upon technical expediency, historical tradition and the organization of the courts of a particular government."—*Ibid.*

CHAPTER VII

Masters and Servants

COINCIDENT with a revolution in the personnel of English political institutions has occurred a shifting of power within the system. Outwardly the classic description of Bagehot remains scarcely unaltered. The King-in-Parliament is still the legal sovereign, ministers of the Crown still depend upon a majority in the House of Commons, and they still assume responsibility for all official acts; but now the fictions which explained the government of Gladstone and Disraeli do not tell the whole story, and new researches are needed to locate the exact repositories of power within the system.

These changes, like most others which confront the people of the twentieth century, are traceable to the two great torrents which swept over the Western world in the nineteenth century—the industrial revolution and political democracy. Both have changed the environment of British government, and it has had to adapt itself or suffer the fate of the dinosaur. The twentieth century has already seen the extinction of many political organisms too inflexible to exist in the new era. The new mechanical age eventually expanded the province of government, and while this movement was stubbornly resisted it became necessary lest the machine develop into an uncontrollable Frankenstein. Public control of the new industrial and social world became absolutely essential. Political democracy, itself growing out of this material revolution, gave governmental institutions a new social context in which to operate. For the technique of oligarchic government, there had to be substituted that of rule by the masses.

The nineteenth century saw the House of Commons wielding power effectively and continuously. Ministries waxed and waned according to the temper of the House, and this power was shared by all the capable members of that body. Some party discipline existed to prevent the House from being simply a weathercock turning this way and that, but still every member was an individual who might assert his independence and snub the whips. Gradually, however, this independence of the private member began to wane. The expansion of the electorate demanded better party organization and more rigid discipline. The increasing business of government put a premium on Parliamentary time which meant more stringent rules of procedure. From a leisurely debating society the House of Commons was being transformed into a business organization. The political instinct of the Irish first sensed this change and appreciated the power it gave them as a well-organized minority group. Their obstructive tactics were met by more procedural rules, necessary to permit the majority to do anything at all. Disraeli is said to have had the prescience to realize that the House of his youth, when argument, oratory, and invective made an impression upon the divisions, was passing, and he retired to the company of the Lords.

The beneficiary of this transformation of the House of Commons was the Cabinet. It monopolized the time of the House, and backed by a disciplined majority it became increasingly the mainspring of the whole governmental machine. The electorate rather than the House of Commons became the ministerial bogeyman, and a defeat in Parliament was followed by a quick appeal to the populace. A victory at the polls meant a new lease on almost dictatorial power. Politicians reserved their best efforts for the platform where they might sway thousands of votes. A former Member of Parliament commenting on

Mr. Balfour's indifferent success as a party leader once wrote, "It is a significant testimony to the declining importance of the House of Commons that Mr. Balfour's dazzling performances in that arena were not considered to atone for his frequent failures on the platform."[1]

Yet paradoxically just at the time the Cabinet was gaining so much power it was losing a great deal, and the final beneficiaries were the permanent civil servants. As the functions of the state increased it became physically impossible for the ministers to wield with any degree of completeness that which they had gained, and they became more and more dependent upon the professional administrator. On the job constantly, he became a new estate of the realm.

Just how far this latter transference has gone cannot be stated with perfect exactitude, for it is a phenomenon of the unwritten constitution and one that varies a good deal according to the personalities and circumstances involved. Some believe that it has gone so far that government by Parliament and Cabinet is merely an elaborately staged puppet show, the motivation and the voices all coming from the unseen civil servants. Mr. Ramsay Muir states this viewpoint very succinctly:

> It is obvious that the Cabinet would be helpless without the Civil Service. But is the reverse statement equally true? Suppose Parliament and the Cabinet to disappear tomorrow. Could government go on? A hundred years ago it probably could not have gone on. Today, almost certainly, it could. If the permanent chiefs of the great Departments of State met at intervals to correlate and dovetail their work, things would run on quite smoothly for quite a long time. This means that bureaucracy has in fact become an indispensable part of our system; indeed the really operative part of it.[2]

[1] A. A. Baumann, *Persons and Politics of the Transition* (London, 1916), p. 62.
[2] *How Britain is Governed* (New York, 1930), p. 36.

In other words, there are fears in Britain that the Civil Service has been transformed into a bureaucracy, a word which has disquieting implications in Anglo-Saxon countries. It has been ably argued that no essential distinction can be drawn between a civil service and a bureaucracy; in fact, the former term was coined by "able and far-sighted politicians" as "a more sympathetic substitute for the many-eyed monster, bureaucracy." [3] While a political scientist may deplore the loose nomenclature applied to governmental organs, he must recognize that in English-speaking countries there is a distinction between civil service and bureaucracy. It is largely a distinction of spirit rather than form. The term "bureaucracy," however innocuous it may be technically, conveys certain sinister implications which Anglo-Saxons dislike. It implies that the administrative branch of the government possesses a mind and will of its own, that it is subject to no effective check by the representative organs of the state, and that all its actions are encumbered with the inefficient, annoying rigmarole called red tape. Mr. Henry Wickham Steed has expressed the distinction in this manner: "The difference between a bureaucracy and a civil service is that the former knows it is the government whereas the latter admits to itself, in the last resort, that its function is to serve the public through the State." [4]

Do these symptoms of bureaucracy fit the British government today? "The word cannot be justified," quoting Muir again, "if these huge staffs of professional administrators are only the agents and servants of directing brains outside of their *cadre*." [5] A reading of the events for the past few years leads one to suspect that there is considerable justification for the use of the word. At least in some departments bureaucratic control is pretty much in evidence constantly, and in others sporadically.

[3] C. J. Friedrich and T. Cole, *op. cit.*, p. 4.
[4] *Through Thirty Years* (New York, 1924), I, 330.
[5] *Op. cit.*, p. 54.

Virtually uncontrolled administration by professional officials is not the novelty in British government that it is sometimes supposed to be. Newspaper editors frequently write as if bureaucracy were entirely a postwar creation. The bureaucratic rule of the Colonial Office throughout most of the Victorian era is an old story: "Mr. Mothercountry" of Charles Buller's satire can be identified in a number of actual officials. It was only when a Joseph Chamberlain occupied the chair of the Secretary of State that the office had policies and programs imposed from above. At other times it carried on in the old grooves. For years the India Office was perhaps even more dominated by the professional administrators than its colonial sister. Here one set of bureaucrats vied with another, the Indian Civil Service, which was the epitome of professionalized administration. They knew the jigsaw puzzle which is India as no minister possibly could, and so they practically had a free hand. When nationalism stirred the sleeping masses and aroused a desire for more than honest administration, then the machine required overhauling, and the politicians were forced to divert some of their time and energies to the designing of a new system which the bureaucrats could handle.

Chamberlain was constantly disturbing the pretty gardens of the bureaucrats. Of his appointment as President of the Board of Trade in Gladstone's second government (1880), his biographer remarks that "fresh air blew through the corridors and freshened the rooms" of that department.[6] The permanent officials had been "entirely in command," but the "new minister was to be no parliamentary mouthpiece ventriloquised by his experts."[7] And so for a time bureaucracy gave way to the energetic politician from Birmingham.

While a large degree of bureaucracy has existed at times

[6] J. L. Garvin, *The Life of Joseph Chamberlain* (London, Macmillan, 1932), I, 411.
[7] *Ibid.*, p. 410.

MASTERS AND SERVANTS 161

in such departments as the Colonial Office, the India Office, and the Board of Trade, its extension to several other departments has been more recent. Throughout most of the nineteenth century the Treasury was actually ruled by the successive Chancellors of the Exchequer. One can hardly imagine Gladstone as window dressing for a staff of professional officials. And some of his successors were equally as forceful. Lord Oxford and Asquith recorded a story of Sir William Harcourt's way with his Treasury staff which scarcely sounds like a cringing minister taking orders from his nominal servants. He wrote:

> Harcourt would even sometimes—in the intervals of browbeating his spendthrift colleagues—take to lecturing his subordinates for their laxity and soft-heartedness; offences from which, to do them justice, they were as a rule conspicuously free. I remember once, in the days when I was Home Secretary and he was Chancellor of the Exchequer, happening to come into his room at the back of the Speaker's Chair. There I found some half-dozen of the highest officials of the Treasury, standing in a row with Sir R. Welby at their head, while Harcourt was pouring out a stream of vitriolic objurations, ending up with the words: "All I can say is that if any firm in the City were run in the way the Treasury is, it would be in the Bankruptcy Court in a week." [8]

But in the past few years the influence of the permanent officials of the Treasury appears to be more pronounced. Perhaps it is because the huge budgets of the postwar era are so much more involved than the relatively simple ones of the Gladstonian period that only men who have spent a lifetime in the constant study of government finance can thread their way to the ultimate results of the figures; or perhaps the margin between solvency and collapse is so slight that experimentation by a vigorous Chancellor of the Exchequer would be suicidal.

Treasury control as applied to the departmental estimates means control by the permanent officials almost

[8] *Memories and Reflections, 1852-1927* (Boston, Little, Brown, 1928), I, 304-5.

entirely, although, of course, major problems can be carried to the Chancellor of the Exchequer or to the Cabinet. Occasionally amusing incidents from among the backstage parleys of the Treasury break out into the open. A classic case was the row which occurred in 1930 over certain expenditures desired by the Admiralty for the monster battleships *H.M.S. Rodney* and *H.M.S. Nelson*. The Treasury, it appears, suggested that as a matter of economy and "as there is going to be no war in many years" these lions of the fleet go to sea with dummy guns. "The Admiralty were unable to take that view," Sir Oswyn A. B. Murray, the Permanent Secretary, later explained. "They felt that if they once gave way to this heresy—that it did not matter whether the guns could fire or not—we should very soon have nothing but a dummy fleet at sea." [9] The Admiralty estimates of 1913 represented a case in which Cabinet intervention was necessary; in fact, they "formed the main and often the sole topic of conversation at fourteen full meetings of the Cabinet. Though the First Lord of the Admiralty was originally in a minority of one the Cabinet ultimately overruled the Treasury." [10] Regarding this incident it was said that the Admiralty wanted six dreadnoughts, the Treasury suggested four, and the Cabinet compromised on eight.

Most differences, however, are threshed out, in camera, between the Treasury officials and the permanent department heads. This is especially true of staff matters. The title "Head of the Civil Service" worn by the Permanent Secretary of the Treasury is no empty phrase. The many cries of lamentation from the lower ranks of the Civil Service raised against the authority of the permanent head and his establishments officers prove this.

The Treasury is not the only department in which policy is frequently dictated by the professional officers. Under the National government there were reports that Foreign

[9] *The New York Times,* October 15, 1932.
[10] Jennings, *op. cit.,* p. 130.

Office policy was often the work of civil servants.[11] This fact is said to account for Britain's non-committal attitude during the recurring crises in the Far East. The presence during the first years of the National government of a foreign minister, Sir John Simon, of one temperament, and a prime minister, Ramsay MacDonald, of a different temperament, both mixing in the international scene, may have compelled the Foreign Office to resolve the two forces into a policy of sorts—colorless but temporarily safe.

The Bridgeman Committee appointed to investigate the Post Office declared recently that "the Secretariat has acquired a dominating power which has imposed on the service a bureaucracy more rigid than that of any other department." [12]

Not only do the professional civil servants control the day-to-day policy of many departments, but they play an important rôle in the preparation of legislation which emanates from their offices. It is safe to say that the detailed provisions of virtually all bills introduced in Parliament are drafted by civil servants, and in some cases the entire program embodied in an important piece of legislation comes from them. The minister sponsors it in Parliament and it is put forward as the handiwork of the government, but frequently that is merely observing the technicalities of legislative procedure. Even the fine and compelling arguments used by the minister in support of the bill are supplied to him by his anonymous subordinates, who must anticipate every point which may be raised in a Parliamentary debate.

A story of quick thinking which saved a minister embarrassment comes from the reminiscences of the late Sir John Kempe, a Treasury official for many years.[13] At one

---

[11] *The New York Times,* October 16, 1932; *Chicago Daily News,* August 23, 1937.
[12] Cmd. 4149 (1932), p. 40.
[13] Sir John Arrow Kempe, *Reminiscences of an Old Civil Servant* (London, 1928), p. 123.

time he was private secretary to the Treasury's Financial Secretary, Lord Frederick Cavendish, and during a debate in which his chief was engaged he remained in the House of Commons until two o'clock in the morning. Believing all was going well, he then went home and retired, but before falling asleep he happened to think of a point which might be raised in debate and on which Lord Frederick might desire some information. Kempe quickly dressed and hurried back to the House. He was none too soon, for almost immediately after his arrival his chief came over to inquire about the very point he had remembered in bed.

With the growing practice of supplementing and implementing acts of Parliament by statutory and provisional orders the influence of the civil servants is increasing. Practically all such orders are penned by them, and while Parliament maintains a technical control over such legislation, in practice they go into effect as drafted by the departments. The scope of many of these orders means that the bureaucracy has a legislative function of no mean importance. Students of British government have frequently pointed out the enormous—to many of them alarming—degree to which Parliament has abdicated its legislative duty in favor of departmental regulation. Writing of this "wholesale transference of control from Parliament to the departments," Professor Laski has said, "Legislation by reference and by delegation has taken the place of the older method which regulated with a jealous precision each item of official activity." [14]

In the past few years particularly this delegation of legislative powers to the departments has provoked a mighty hue and cry. Lord Chief Justice Hewart's *The New Despotism* purported to reveal a bureaucracy wielding powers uncontrolled by either Parliament or courts, and other critical books have been mentioned above in connection with the inquiry of the Committee on

---

[14] Harold J. Laski, "The Growth of Administrative Discretion," *Journal of Public Administration*, April, 1923, p. 92.

Ministers' Powers.[15] It will be recalled that the Committee found the trend toward increased administrative power inevitable and that the problem was one of safeguards rather than that of restoring an earlier order.

It is quite apparent that the Civil Service has become more than merely a corps of administrators faithfully executing rules which their political chiefs have declared in ministerial policies and statutes of the realm. Civil servants are the authors as well as the executors of many of these policies. Numerous programs of their own find embodiment in acts of Parliament. Principal permanent officials become a legislative chamber—silent but effective notwithstanding. The extent to which the permanent staff of any department may control policy, administrative or legislative, depends considerably upon the character of the minister at the head of the office. A forceful politician may still dominate his department. Its policies will be his—actually and technically. But less intrepid leaders will become little more than the mouthpieces of their subordinates.

The power of the bureaucracy naturally varies inversely with the strength of the ministry. If a considerable number of the ministers are new and inexperienced in holding office they will be forced to lean heavily upon the permanent officials, or a party forming a government for the first time, such as Labor in 1924, will find itself very dependent upon the Civil Service. On the other hand, the bureaucracy will play a less important rôle when a considerable proportion of the ministers are distinguished political personalities and experienced in the problems of managing public departments. Haldane, Curzon, and Lloyd George are examples of ministers who so dominated their offices that departmental policies were their own. More frequently, it appears, the political helmsman is unable to effect a radical change in the course of departmental policy. Even weak ministers, though, have a

[15] See above, Chapter VI, p. 136.

veto over policies of their permanent officials, and civil servants cannot proceed with projects in the realm of high policy over ministerial opposition. The bureaucracy in England is still less influential than it is across the Channel, and there are several reasons for this. The venerable tradition in Britain that policy should be controlled by the "amateur" politicians is still strong, while in France bureaucratic control has been common since the days of the Bourbons.[16] Of the days since 1789 it has been said, "Dynasties, flags, and regimes passed away; the Bureaucracy neither died nor surrendered." [17] Traditions like these die hard. Then the longevity of British cabinets as compared with that of French ministries enables the political heads to become masters of their departments and to initiate policies which may not always accord with the views of the civil servants. In France the ordinarily short time during which a minister occupies his office makes him far more dependent upon his subordinates. He no sooner has mastered the intricacies of the office than the mood of the Chamber of Deputies changes and he is plunged into the bartering characteristic of a Cabinet reconstruction or he is definitely an ex-minister. The exigencies of politics have also made the French minister more important as a Parliamentary leader than as an administrator, while the British system places much more emphasis upon the executive and administrative features of Cabinet membership. The British minister can count on his Parliamentary majority remaining fairly secure for at least two or three years, so it is not incumbent upon him to be feeling the pulse of the legislative chambers

---

[16] Lord Grey of Fallodon wrote: "His [a minister's] business is not to be an expert, but to be trained in capacity for public affairs. The theory and practice of parliamentary government is not that of government by experts, but by men of general experience and proved capacity presiding over experts who are the civil servants in our public affairs."—*Op. cit.*, I, 2.

[17] A. Guerard, *Beyond Hatred* (New York, 1925), p. 26. Quoted by Walter R. Sharp in "Public Personnel Management in France," *Civil Service Abroad*, p. 83.

every few hours. In addition, England has been spared the ministerial interregnums which frequently devolve the government of France upon the bureaucracy. Cabinet changes are complete and definite and do not involve the days—and sometimes weeks—of conferring at the Élysée while the civil servants carry on. It is evident that the French bureaucracy could rule almost indefinitely, and that knowledge gives it a self-assurance which it does not hesitate to express. Premier Gaston Doumergue's inclusion of civil service reform in his program of constitutional reconstruction in France was a recognition of the grip which the administrative branch has upon the machinery of the Third Republic.[18]

But despite those features of British government which enable ministers to check bureaucratic control, the growth of power of the Civil Service in recent years is unmistakable. It is becoming more and more difficult for the amateur politician to be an effective administrator and even in legislation his dependence upon subordinates is increasing. "When Lord Balfour became President of the Council in 1925 he told Mr. Baldwin that Cabinet business was three or four times as great as when he first took Cabinet office in 1886." [19] To some who view this trend with alarm the remedy lies in the adoption of machinery which will permit Parliament to have more effective supervision of the administrative branch of the government—the development of a committee system, for example. Undoubtedly a good deal of talent on the back benches goes to waste, but whether cabinet government can permit a large measure of diffused authority is an open question. The tendency has always been in the opposite direction.

Partly to cushion the contact between administrators and public in a nation where resentment is frequently the

[18] M. Doumergue temporized too long after the crisis of February, 1934, and the civil service statute so frequently proposed remains, in the words of Dr. Herman Finer, "the will-o'-the-wisp of French politics."—*The Theory and Practice of Modern Government*, II, 1321.

[19] Jennings, *op. cit.*, p. 193.

natural reaction to governmental interference with the individual, advisory committees have been created in connection with a considerable number of acts and exist more or less informally in several departments. Knowledge that representative people outside government service have been consulted on problems of administration results in a more favorable reception for regulations. "Committees are an invaluable instrument for breaking administrative measures on to the back of the public," Sir Arthur Salter has said.[20]

The civil servants themselves have not been particularly responsible for their own aggrandizement. The growth of public activities and the increasing complexity and specialization of government have thrust new duties upon them and forced them to assume control. "It is not a matter of bureaucratic invasion or administrative arrogance," Professor Ernest Barker has said. "By the authority of Parliament, and under the compulsion of the needs of the political community, they have been drawn into new activities. Not their own motion, but the general motion of politics, has enlarged their duties and widened their powers." [21] The limits of the ability of the average minister to control effectively his whole department with its thousands of employees and multitude of activities are soon reached, and beyond them his chief subordinates must assume command. The minister can only see a limited number of papers and memoranda, and he can only be at one place at one time. A capable minister can so organize his work and so infuse his staff with his views that his influence carries beyond the human limits of his own activities, but there remains much in which the civil servants must take the initiative and must make the actual decisions.

With the increasing appreciation of the important rôle

---

[20] Sir William Beveridge, *The Development of the Civil Service* (London, 1922), p. 220. See above, Chapter VI, pp. 152-53.
[21] "The Home Civil Service," *The British Civil Servant*, p. 30.

of the civil servants in the formation and execution of policy, there is some question of the desirability of continuing the virtually absolute anonymity of their opinions. Certainly for the historian the memoranda of these officers would be of incalculable value in illuminating many a dark corner. Surmises could frequently be set down as facts. But there are other sides to this question. In a letter to *The Times* the late Lord Grey expressed some pertinent views on this subject. He wrote:

> May I add that it seems to me very undesirable to publish the minutes and memoranda of permanent officials in Government Departments? They are not authoritative documents. The writers of them have no responsibility for ultimate decisions and policy. If they are to be published the prospect of their publication will hamper the freedom of permanent officials in expressing their views to the Ministers who are at the head of their Departments. This would not be in the public interest.[22]

Lord Grey made a good point for continuing the present practice. If important memoranda of civil servants are published with any frequency the tendency will be to write them with an eye to that fact, and to do so would impair their value to ministers. Ministers today can rely upon the advice of their subordinates as being the opinions of conscientious officials, uncolored by any fears or hopes as to how posterity will judge them. Bringing their advice into the open would also endanger the completely nonpolitical status of the permanent officials, and certainly attempts would be made to control them or make them responsible in some way for the advice tendered. This would introduce a complexity into government that well may be avoided. Perhaps a compromise might be reached by allowing historians to use such material after the personalities and events concerned have passed from the stage. It would then be of interest to few except the students of history. At any rate, to modify the present rule would work more

[22] November 21, 1932.

harm than good.[23] The civil servant had best remain true, like the Franciscan, to the triple vow of poverty, anonymity, and obedience.[24] The rôle of the modern civil servant is not a particularly easy one. The principal subordinates of a minister frequently must work long hours so that the chief will be prepared for an important conference or Parliamentary debate, and if their labors are crowned with success the laurel wreaths go to the minister. They must adapt themselves to working with diverse types of men—country gentlemen, trade union organizers, industrialists, or any sort that the vagaries of politics elevate to ministerial office. They must restrain their impatience when serving under a new minister whose business knowledge may have been gained in managing a family estate or representing the interests of fellow craftsmen and who is tackling a government department for the first time. As Lord Oxford and Asquith wrote, "The position of a permanent civil servant, especially when he has reached the upper ranks of the hierarchy, is one which calls for a certain amount of flexibility in addition to administrative ability." Regarding the problem of adjustment to a new minister he said:

The new head may turn out to be a mere figure-head; he may be a good, honest mediocrity, anxious to learn the technique of the office and to give full weight to the judgment of his expert staff; he may be by nature a meddler and a muddler, or what is even more troublesome to his subordinates, a man of the best of intentions with limited visions and an obstinate will: he may be, as Campbell-Bannerman once said to me of a colleague of ours, *"Maximus in minimis, minimus in maximis."* Or, on the other hand—for there are infinite varieties of possibility—he may be, if not a heaven-born administrator, at any rate one who will never let his

[23] It is Dr. Herman Finer's opinion that the "modern system of ministerial responsibility and of changing Cabinets, unequivocally demands that Civil Servants shall do their work without personal public blame or praise for policy.:..."—*The Theory and Practice of Modern Government,* II, 1182.
[24] Beveridge, *op. cit.,* p. 231.

office down in the Cabinet or the House of Commons. Who can tell in advance? And the task of prophecy becomes more difficult when the new minister comes with a reputation already made in other fields: such for instance, to take wholly dissimilar cases, as Cornewall Lewis, or Morley, or Randolph Churchill, or John Burns.[25]

Lord Curzon once remarked that he doubted if ministers ever really appreciated what they owe to the Civil Service. "We are not half grateful enough for what they do," he said. "We expect them to be always on the spot, always cheerful and attentive, at the very same time when they may be having all sorts of troubles of their own; domestic worries; financial anxieties; ill health." [26] However, practically every British statesman has recognized the debt he owes to his subordinate staff, and at some time or other he pays tribute to their services. Let a statement of Chamberlain's be regarded as typical of these tributes.

...When first I commenced, I found myself face to face with a hundred questions, many of them involving many technical details of which I humbly confess I was profoundly ignorant; and if I was saved from making mistakes which would have been humiliating, I owe it to the care and knowledge and intelligence of the permanent officials of my department, who have in so many cases to supply or to conceal the deficiencies of their parliamentary chiefs.[27]

The masters and the servants in present-day British government cannot be identified without qualifications. "It is often difficult," says Ramsay Muir, "to determine where the real initiative, and the effective power of decision, actually lie in practice." [28] The ministers are nominally the masters of the current political scene. They owe a responsibility to the House of Commons, but the mastery of the latter is not as real as in former days, al-

---

[25] *Op. cit.*, I, 298.
[26] Earl of Ronaldshay, *The Life of Lord Curzon* (London, 1926), III, 206.
[27] Garvin, *op. cit.*, I, 410.
[28] *Op. cit.*, p. 54.

though as the reflector of popular opinion it occasionally forces the strongest of Cabinets to mend their ways. The case of Sir Samuel Hoare and his Ethiopian bargain will doubtless remind Cabinets for some time to come that Parliament and the public behind it are still alive and opinionated. However, for the most part, the ministers are not only the nominal but the actual masters of general policy. Occasionally, because of the ineptitude or incapacity of a minister, control in a government department virtually passes to the permanent officials, but this condition is not so probable today as it was two or three generations ago. No politician is likely to reach Cabinet rank unless he is a man of ability and personality—a natural leader—and no branch of government in these modern times is so long out of the glare of publicity that it affords a cozy retreat for an incompetent with the proper connections.

The ministers, though, must confine their mastery to general policy. A great deal of governmental work, that which is called administration, must be left to the Civil Service. The dividing line between the executive work of ministers and the administration of the permanent officials is not a deep, straight trench. The two fields overlap, and where the line will be drawn in any particular service depends upon local circumstances and the personalities involved.

Increasingly in the future it will be the office of the minister to provide a connecting link between Parliament and the administrative department. The minister, recognizing that he cannot manage a department in the manner of his predecessors a half century ago, will find one of his chief duties to be that of interpreting public sentiment to the permanent officials. To his Parliamentary colleagues, who frequently feel isolated from the administrative work of government, the minister will bring the plans and projects of his department.

The administrative work has increased immensely in importance. Whereas it formerly consisted principally of the application of rules to situations and persons subject to governmental regulation, it today includes that, on a much enlarged scale, and also the performance of services which call for the exercise of intelligent discretion and long-range planning. "In these service functions," Professor Robson has said, "the official is less concerned to administer law than to promote energetic and far-reaching projects based on plans which he himself must create." [29] Concretely the difference may be illustrated by citing the Factory Acts as examples of the old-style regulation and the housing projects of the Ministry of Health as a sample of the new service required.

Some recognition of the need for officials freed sufficiently from departmental administration to plan and study on a general and long-time basis is found in the appointments of Sir Horace Wilson and Sir Frederick Leith-Ross as economic and financial advisers to the Treasury and, more recently, of Sir Robert Vansittart as Foreign Office adviser on high policy. This small group of permanent advisory officials is almost certain to grow larger.

In view of the importance of this new administrative work in the lives of the citizens in these modern, interdependent nations the personnel of the Civil Service is a matter of great moment. Dull and unimaginative personnel will naturally mean ineffective and costly public services; intelligent and creative officials can take great strides toward that more abundant life which politicians offer as their objective.

It has already been stated that England entered the period of rapid social change equipped with a high-grade corps of professional administrators. While many other countries were still struggling along with a service of largely political hacks who came and went as parties alternated in office, England had abandoned patronage and induced a large proportion of the best products of her schools and universities to enter public service. With the achievement of a civil service renowned for its integrity

[29] W. A. Robson, "The Public Service," *The British Civil Servant*, p. 19.

and devotion to duty, some Englishmen are wondering whether this administrative evolution has proceeded far enough. They are wondering specifically whether the state is today recruiting an officialdom attuned to the tempo of modern Britain and alive to its problems.

A considerable change in the personnel of the upper ranks of the Civil Service has occurred since the World War. By the route of open competition or promotion men and women are entering the Administrative Class who a generation or two back would not have been eligible because of the lack of educational opportunities or service traditions. However, this change is not comparable to the revolution which has occurred in the personnel of Parliament or the councils of local governments where coal miners, railwaymen, and tradesmen sit with country gentlemen, captains of industry, and barristers.

No one advocates a lowering of the high intellectual standards for admittance into the Civil Service, but there is a large body of opinion which feels that the area of selection should be broadened, in keeping with the general democratization of British institutions, and care should be taken to insure that recruits are people of energy, vision, and liberal inclinations. The former is being accomplished to some degree by the extension of educational opportunities to classes formerly deprived of them. Many young men of lower class origin are going to Oxford and Cambridge on scholarships, and even more are seeking university educations in London or the provincial towns. However, those unable to go to the older universities are handicapped in entering the Civil Service because the examinations still tend to favor an education at Oxford or Cambridge. A remedying of this situation would do much to broaden the area of selection, and in view of the emphasis upon social sciences at London and some of the provincial universities there is no justification for the refusal to give their students an equal opportunity for admittance into public service.

Securing personnel of the proper temperament, energy, and vision for the new social service state is a more difficult problem than that of breaking down its caste character. These qualities are to be found among individuals from all classes of society. Many of the permanent officials of the past have been men of highest intelligence and creative ability. The problem today is that of selecting from among many intellectually keen candidates those who will develop into strong, resourceful officers instead of timid bureaucrats. The open competitive examination, which strains out only the intellectually inferior, makes this somewhat difficult. Open competition, however, is too valuable a protection against patronage and nepotism to be abandoned. And fortunately British experience indicates a fairly high correlation between intelligence and administrative ability. Part of the solution seems to be a more careful employment of the *viva voce* section of the examination—not by raising the marks allotted to it, for they are excessively high now, but by making it more objective and formal and less haphazard. Special attention to the training of young officers will be helpful, too. No talent appearing in the lower ranks should be overlooked, of course.

The criticism directed against the Civil Service in recent years, some of it deserved and most of it not, has awakened Englishmen to a realization of the important place which administration occupies in their governmental system. The problems connected with administrative personnel—the character of officials, their selection and training—are as important to progressive government as the selection of honest and intelligent members of Parliament. In both fields of public service, the political and the permanent, England has valuable traditions upon which to build. With the increasing democratization of all kinds of public service there is no need to sacrifice the virtues in the legacy of the governing classes, for they can be employed—and, indeed, are essential—in the state of tomorrow.

APPENDIX I

Administrative Class Examination

Section A.—Candidates are to take up all the subjects in this section.

1. Essay 100
2. English 100
3. Present Day 100
4. Viva Voce 300

Section B.—Optional Subjects.—Candidates are allowed to take up subjects in this section up to a total of 700 marks.

History

5. British History, Period I 200
6. British History, Period II 200
7. European History, *either* Period I or Period II 200
8. European History, Period III 200

Law, Philosophy, Politics, and Economics

9. Private Law, Part I.. 200
10. Private Law, Part II 200
11. Jurisprudence 100
12. Constitutional Law.. 100
13. Roman Law 200
14. International Law .. 100
15. Metaphysics, Paper I 100
16. Metaphysics, II 100
17. Metaphysics, III 100
18. Moral Philosophy, Paper I 100
19. Moral Philosophy, II 100
20. Logic 100
21. Psychology 100
22. Experimental Psychology 100
23. Political Theory 100
24. Political Organisation 100
25. International Relations 100
26. General Economics.. 200
27. Industry and Trade 100
28. Money, Banking, and Exchange 100
29. Public Finance 100
30. Social Economics ... 100
31. Economic History .. 100
32. Economic Statistics.. 100

Mathematics and Science

33. Lower Pure Mathematics 200	45. Lower Physiology .. 200
34. Lower Applied Mathematics 200	46. Higher Physiology .. 300
	47. Lower Zoology 200
35. Higher Mathematics 300	48. Higher Zoology 300
36. Astronomy 200	49. Engineering 400
37. Lower Chemistry ... 200	50. Geography 400
38. Higher Chemistry... 300	51. General Anthropology 100
39. Lower Physics 200	
40. Higher Physics 300	52. Special Anthropology, consisting of either Social Anthropology or Physical Anthropology. 100
41. Lower Botany 200	
42. Higher Botany 300	
43. Lower Geology 200	
44. Higher Geology 300	

Language and Civilisations

53. Old and Middle English 100	69. French Literature .. 100
54. English Literature, Period 1 200	70. German Language .. 200
	71. German History 100
55. English Literature, Period 2 200	72. German Literature.. 100
	73. Spanish or Italian Language 200
56. Welsh Civilisation .. 200	
57. Greek Translation .. 100	74. Spanish or Italian History 100
58. Greek Composition.. 100	
59. Greek History 100	75. Spanish or Italian Literature 100
60. Greek Literature ... 100	
61. Latin Translation .. 100	76. Russian Language .. 200
62. Latin Composition.. 100	77. Russian History 100
63. Roman History 100	78. Russian Literature 100
64. Latin Literature ... 100	79. Arabic Language ... 200
65. Classical Archaeology, Paper I 100	80. Arabic History 100
	81. Arabic Literature ... 100
66. Classical Archaeology, Paper II 100	82. Persian Language 200
	83. Persian History 100
67. French Language ... 200	84. Persian Literature .. 100
68. French History 100	

APPENDIX II

Comparison between Administrative Class Remuneration and Outside Business

(From *Royal Commission on the Civil Service, 1929-31, Minutes of Evidence*, App. VIII, p. 66.)

A. University Men entering Business:
  1. Average entrant may expect to reach £1,000 mark at about thirty years of age.
  2. Majority reach £2,000 mark at about forty years of age.
  3. Large minority may reach £3,000 mark at later ages.
  4. Small minority reach much higher salaries.

B. University Men entering the Administrative Class:
  1. Average entrant will reach £570 mark at thirty years of age.
  2. Most entrants reach £1,190 mark at forty years of age.
  3. At later ages—33% reach £1,240; 33% reach £1,580; 20% reach £1,900; 7% reach £2,475; 7% reach £3,400.
  4. None beyond £3,500.

APPENDIX III

Composition of the Staff Side of the National Whitley Council

The National Staff Side is composed of the following groups, the majority of which are federations of several or many staff associations:

Union of Post Office Workers	115,159
Civil Service Confederation	100,966
Post Office Engineering Union	27,084
Sub-Postmasters' Federation	16,124
Institution of Professional Civil Servants	11,632
Federation of Post Office Supervising Officers	8,314
	279,279

SELECTED BIBLIOGRAPHY

I. GENERAL

Finer, Herman. *The Theory and Practice of Modern Government.* New York, The Dial Press, 1932. 2 vols.
Gaus, John M. *Great Britain: A Study of Civic Loyalty.* Chicago, University of Chicago Press, 1929.
Gretton, R. H. *A Modern History of the English People, 1880–1922.* New York, The Dial Press, 1930.
Halévy, Élie. *A History of the English People.* New York, Harcourt, Brace, 1924. 3 vols.
―――. *A History of the English People: Epilogue.* London, E. Benn, 1929-34. 2 vols.
Laski, Harold J. *A Grammar of Politics.* London, G. Allen & Unwin, 1925.
Lowell, A. Lawrence. *The Government of England.* New York, Macmillan, 1909. 2 vols.
Marriott, Sir John A. R. *How England is Governed.* London, H. Milford, Oxford University Press, 1928.
―――. *England Since Waterloo.* London, Methuen, 1914.
Muir, Ramsay. *How Britain Is Governed.* New York, Richard R. Smith, 1930.
Ogg, Frederic A. *English Government and Politics.* New York, Macmillan, 1936.
Smellie, K. B. *A Hundred Years of English Government.* New York, Macmillan, 1937.

II. PARLIAMENT AND THE CABINET

Allyn, Emily. *Lords versus Commons: A Century of Conflict and Compromise, 1830–1930.* New York, Century, 1931.
Baumann, A. A. *Persons and Politics of the Transition.* London, Macmillan, 1916.

Farquharson, Robert. *The House of Commons from Within.* London, 1912.
Ilbert, Sir Courtney. *Parliament: Its History, Constitution and Practice.* New York, Holt, 1911.
Jennings, William Ivor. *Parliamentary Reform.* London, Gollancz, 1934.
———. *Cabinet Government.* New York, Macmillan, 1936.
MacDonagh, Michael. *The Pageant of Parliament.* London, T. F. Unwin, 1921. 2 vols.
Morley, John (Lord). *The Life of William Ewart Gladstone.* New York, Macmillan, 1903.
Oxford and Asquith, Earl of. *Fifty Years of Parliament.* London, Cassell, 1926. 2 vols.
———. *Memories and Reflections, 1852–1927.* Boston, Little, Brown, 1928. 3 vols.
Pollard, A. F. *The Evolution of Parliament.* New York, Longmans Green, 1920.
Seymour, Charles. *Electoral Reform in England and Wales.* New Haven, Yale University Press, 1915.
Studies of Yesterday, by a Privy Councillor. London, 1928.

III. THE CIVIL SERVICE

Allen, Carleton Kemp. *Bureaucracy Triumphant.* London, H. Milford, Oxford University Press, 1931.
Beveridge, Sir William. *The Public Service in War and Peace.* London, Constable, 1920.
Burns, C. Delisle. *Whitehall.* London, H. Milford, Oxford University Press, 1921.
Carr, Cecil T. *Delegated Legislation.* Cambridge, The University Press, 1921.
Committee on the Selection and Training of Candidates for the Indian Civil Service. *Report, 1854. Parliamentary Papers, 1855.* (Macaulay Report.)
Committee on Ministers' Powers. *Report, 1932.* London, H. M. Stationery Office, 1932. Cmd. 4060, 1932.
Demetriadi, Sir Stephen. *Inside a Government Office.* London, Cassell, 1921.
———. *A Reform for the Civil Service.* London, Cassell, 1921.

BIBLIOGRAPHY

Eaton, Dorman B. *Civil Service in Great Britain: A History of Abuses and Reforms and Their Bearing upon American Politics.* New York, Harpers, 1880.

Emden, C. S. *The Civil Servant in the Law and the Constitution.* London, Stevens, 1923.

Evans, Dorothy. *Women and the Civil Service.* London, Pitman, 1934.

Fiddes, Sir George V. *The Dominions and Colonial Offices.* Whitehall Series. London, Putnam, 1926.

Finer, Herman. *The British Civil Service.* London, Fabian Society and Allen & Unwin, 1937.

Heath, Sir Thomas Little. *The Treasury.* Whitehall Series. London, Putnam, 1927.

Hewart, Rt. Hon. Lord Hewart of Bury. *The New Despotism.* London, E. Benn, 1929.

Joint Committee on the Organization of Permanent Civil Service. *Report, November 23, 1853. Parliamentary Papers, 1854.* (Trevelyan-Northcote Report.)

Lambie, Morris B. *The British Civil Service Personnel Administration.* Washington, Government Printing Office, 1929.

Machinery of Government Committee. *Report of the Machinery of Government Committee.* London, H. M. Stationery Office, 1918. Cmd. 9230, 1918. (Haldane Report.)

Macrae-Gibson, J. H. *The Whitley System in the Civil Service.* London, The Fabian Society, 1922.

Moses, Robert. *The Civil Service of Great Britain.* New York, Columbia University Press, 1914.

Mustoe, N. E. *The Law and Organization of the British Civil Service,* London, Pitman, 1932.

Robson, William A. *From Patronage to Proficiency in the Civil Service.* London, Fabian Society, 1922.

———. *Justice and Administrative Law: A Study of the British Constitution.* London, Macmillan, 1928.

——— (ed.). *The British Civil Servant.* London, G. Allen & Unwin, 1937.

Royal Commission on the Civil Service. Fourth Report, 1914. Cmd. 7338, 1914. (MacDonnell Report.)

———. *Fifth Report.* Cmd. 7748, 1914.

———. *Sixth Report.* Cmd. 7832, 1915.

Royal Commission on the Civil Service. Report, 1929–31.
London, H. M. Stationery Office, 1931. Cmd. 3909, 1931.
(Tomlin Report.)

Shepherd, Edwin Colston. *The Fixing of Wages in Government Employment.* London, Methuen, 1923.

Society of Civil Servants. *The Development of the Civil Service.* London, P. S. King, 1922.

Walker, Harvey. *Training Public Employees in Great Britain.* New York, McGraw-Hill, 1935.

White, Leonard D. *Whitley Councils in the British Civil Service.* Chicago, University of Chicago Press, 1933.

―――. "The British Civil Service," *Civil Service Abroad.* New York, McGraw-Hill, 1935.

Willis, John. *The Parliamentary Powers of English Government Departments.* Cambridge, Harvard University Press, 1933.

Index

ABERDEEN, Lord, 38
Abstractor Class. *See* Assistant Clerks
Administrative Class, 80, 81, 82, 88, 99; annual leaves, 96; appointment to, 86; education for, 101*ff.*, 113; examination for, 85, 112; personnel, 100*ff.*, 139, 154, 174; promotions, 96, 106; remuneration, 93, 150
Administrative Reform, 10
Administrative reorganization, 5*ff.*
Admiralty, 4, 162
Advisory committees, 152, 167
Allen, C. K., 136
American Bar Association's Special Committee on Administrative Law, 144*n*.
Anderson, Sir John, 94
Army Council, 23
Assistant Clerks, 50
Atholl, Duchess of, 53*n*.

BAILLIE, James Black, 53*n*.
Baker, Harold Trevor, 52*n*.
Baldwin, Lord (Stanley), 69, 72, 75
Balfour, Lord, 11, 158
Ballot Act (1872), 22
Barker, Ernest, quoted, 168
Baumann, A. A., 158*n*.
Beveridge, Sir William, 168*n*., 170*n*.
Birkett, F. G., 131*n*., 151*n*.
Blachly, F. F., 129*n*., 143*n*.
Boerner, Alfred V., Jr., 112*n*.
Bolingbroke, Lord, 16
Booth, Alfred Allen, 52*n*.
Boutwood, Arthur, 52*n*.
Boy Copyists, 50
"Brain Trust," 77, 78
Bridgeman Committee on the Post Office, 151, 163
British Broadcasting Corporation, 6

Bromley, John, 53*n*.
Bromley, R. M., 24
Brown, W. J., 122
Bullock, Sir Christopher, 110*n*.
Bunbury, Sir Henry, 121*n*.
Bureaucracy, 135*ff.*, 159, 164, 166; in France, 166

CABINET, 157; growth in size, 4; inner, 4; membership in, 69*ff.*; secretariat, 6; war, 4
Cambridge, University of, 83, 86, 87, 102, 103, 109, 174; Union, 68
Carlyle, Thomas, 29
Cash, William, 53*n*.
Chadwick, Edwin, 25
Chamberlain, Joseph, 160, 171
Chartists, 21
Churchill, Winston, 69
Civil list, 23
Civil service, 10; ages of entrants, 84; anonymity of, 168; arbitration in, 133; code of ethics, 110; criticism of, 135*ff.*, 146; examinations for, 85; ex-service men in, 124; growth of, 5, 30; head of, 121; increasing power of, 167; integration with educational system, 83; numbers in, 115; organization of, 42, 46, 49, 80, 116, 118*ff.*; personnel of, 123, 154, 173; Playfair Commission on, 45, 48; prohibition of political activity in, 95; promotion in, 106; public confidence in, 44, 147*ff.*; recognition of services in, 98; recruitment for, 52, 123, 148, 174; reform of, 23*ff.*; report of Northcote and Trevelyan on, 33*ff.*; resignations from, 93; Ridley Commission on, 48, 50; Royal (MacDonnell) Commission, 1912-15, on, 50, 116, 118; Royal

INDEX

Civil Service— (*Cont'd*)
(Tomlin) Commission, 1929-31, on, 53*ff.*, 88, 93, 99, 108, 122, 125, 131, 149; security of tenure, 95; select committee (1860) on, 40; select committee (1873) on, 43; training in, 175; unionism in, 127; war period, 117
Civil Service Arbitration Tribunal, 133
Civil Service Clerical Association, 120
Civil Service Commissioners, 39, 88, 112, 124; certificate of, 40
Clerical Class, 84, 123
Clynes, John Robert, 52*n*.
Cole, Taylor, 84*n*., quoted, 153*n*., 155*n*., 159*n*.
Colonial Civil Service, 108*n*.
Colonial Land and Emigration Office, 32
Colonial Office, 32, 40, 160
Commission of Inquiry on Governmental Personnel, 15*n*.
Committee of Imperial Defense, 6, 7
Committee on Ministers' Powers, 138, 139, 140, 141, 143, 144, 145, 146, 155, 164
Consular Service, 112
Controller of Establishments, 122
Copyhold, Enclosure and Tithe Commission, 32
Corruption, in elections, 21
Crimean War, 22, 23, 39
Crown Proceedings Bill, 146
Curzon, Lord, 165, 171

Dalziel, Lord, 59
David, Paul T., 80*n*.
Delegated legislation, 138*ff.*, 164
Departmental autonomy, 119
Departmental classes, 119
Devonshire, Duke of, 52*n*.
Diplomatic Service, 83, 107, 113
Disraeli, Benjamin, 71, 157
Donoughmore, Earl of, 138
Dublin, University of, 102

Eastern Cadetships, 102
East India Company, 35, 39
Eaton, Dorman B., quoted, 45
Economic Advisory Council, 8
Eden, Anthony, 73
Edinburgh, University of, 102

Electricity Commissioners, 6
Elliott, W. Y., quoted, 78, 86
Established civil servants, 57*n*.
Establishments Department, 121, 122
Evans, Dorothy, quoted, 88*n*.
Evelyn, Lucy Anne, 52*n*.
Executive Class, 84, 123

Factory Acts, 173
Fairlie, John A., 153*n*.
Finer, Herman, quoted, 87, 90, 112, 167*n*., 170*n*.; 92*n*., 107*n*., 109*n*.
First Division Clerks, 49, 50
Fisher, Sir Warren, 81, 96, 99, 108, 110, 122, 131, 149, 150
Foreign Office, 40, 73, 83, 107, 110, 162; examination for, 89, 112
Franchise, extension of, 19
Francs Case, 110, 149
Fremantle, Sir Thomas Francis, 25
French Civil Service, 91
Friedrich, Carl J., 84*n*.; quoted, 153*n*., 155*n*., 159*n*.

Garvin, J. L., quoted, 160*n*.
Geddes Committee on National Expenditure, 7*n*.
General election, of 1906, 10; of 1935, 64, 65
General strike, 128
German Civil Service, 90; code of ethics in, 111*n*.
Gladstone, Herbert, 70
Gladstone, William Ewart, 32, 37, 39, 71, 101, 161
Gladstone Committee, 118
Glover, Edward Auchmuty, 21
Goldstone, Frank Walter, 53*n*.
Gort, Viscount, 23
Gould, Barbara Ayrton, 53*n*.
Governing classes, 61, 74, 82
Graham, Major, 25
Graham, Sir James, 38
Granet, Sir William Guy, 52*n*.
Gretton, R. H., quoted, 12*n*.
Grey, Earl, of Fallodon, 72; quoted, 166*n*., 169
Guinness Agreement, 124
Gwyer, M. L., 110

Haileybury School, 32, 36
Haldane, Elizabeth Sanderson, 52*n*.
Haldane, Lord, 165

INDEX

Haldane Report. *See* Machinery of Government Committee
Hamilton, Mary Agnes, 53n.
Hankey, Sir Maurice, 6, 97n.
Harcourt, Sir William, 161
Henderson, Arthur, 71
Henry VIII clause, 142, 146
Hewart, Lord Chief Justice, 136, 146
Higgs, Henry, quoted, 120, 121n.
Hill, Rowland, 25
Hoare, Sir Samuel, J. G., 52n., 73, 171
Holt, Richard Durning, 52n.
Hore-Belisha, Leslie, 23
"Hot Oil" cases, 141, 142
Houghton, A. L. N. D., quoted, 88
House of Commons, 3, 157; civil service representatives in, 129; Communist party in, 65; Conservative party in, 60ff., 65; Independent Labor party in, 65; Independent Liberal party in, 65; Labor party in, 64, 65; Liberal party in, 63; members of, 61ff.; National Labor party in, 65; reform of, 17ff.
House of Lords, 3

Illegal Practices Prevention Act (1883), 22
Indian Civil Service, 102, 108n., 160; reform of, 35
India Office, 41, 160
Industrial Court, 120
Industrial Courts Act (1919), 133
Inskip, Sir Thomas W. H., 7
Interdepartmental committees, 7
Intermediate Clerical Class, 50

Jackson, Sir Percy Richard, 53n.
Jennings, W. Ivor, 7n., 8n., quoted, 167n.
Joint Consultative Committee, 94n., 128
Jowett, Rev. Benjamin, 34

Kekewich, Sir G. W., 150
Kempe, Sir John A., 163
Kingsley, J. Donald, 95n.

Labor government, 12; civil service and, 130, 165
Labor party, composition of, 65; ministers, 74; and Parliamentary reform, 4, 5
Lansbury, George, 71
Lansdowne, Lord, on size of Cabinet, 4
Laski, Harold J., quoted, 65, 69n., 72, 97, 153, 164
Leith-Ross, Sir Frederick, 173
Lindsay, A. D., 100, 105n.
Lloyd George, David, 4, 6, 69, 165; quoted, 97n.
London, University of. *See* University of London
London Passenger Transport Board, 6, 150
Lowe, Mary Eveline, 53n.
Lowe, Robert, 36
Lowell, A. Lawrence, 28n., 36n.; quoted, 27n.
Lowther, James William. *See* Ullswater, Viscount
Lytton, Earl of, 124

MacAlister, Sir Donald, 52n.
Macaulay, Lord, 29, 35, 36
MacDonagh, M., quoted, 21-22
MacDonald, Malcolm, 70
MacDonald, J. Ramsay, 71, 163; quoted, 1, 66
MacDonnell Commission. *See* Civil Service, Royal Commission on (1912-15)
MacDonnell, Lord, 50, 52
Machinery of Government Committee, 4, 7, 153
Mackenzie, Sir Kenneth A. M., 53n.
Macrae-Gibson, J. H., quoted, 128n.
Marriott, Sir John, 136
Marshall-Hall, Sir Edward, 67
Marx, Fritz Morstein, quoted, 111n., 129n.
Matheson, Percy Ewing, 52n.
May Committee, 7n.
Meiklejohn, Sir Roderick, 105; quoted, 85
Merivale, Herman, 25, 28
Military services, reform of, 22
Mill, John Stuart, 35, 37
Minister for the Co-ordination of Defense, 7
Ministers, functions of, 172; judicial powers of, 144; legislative powers of, 139ff.
Morant, Sir Robert, 154
Morley, Lord, quoted, 38

Morning Post, quoted, 135, 149
Moses, Robert, 30*n.;* quoted, 41-42, 52
Mosher, William E., 95*n.*
Muir, Ramsay, 99, 109; quoted, 158, 159, 171
Murray, Sir Evelyn, 95*n.*
Murray, Sir Oswyn A. B., 162
Mustoe, N. E., 95*n.*

NATIONAL government, 73
National Labor party, 65
National Liberal party, 63
National Whitley Council, 118, 128, 131, 132; reorganization committee of, 55, 118; staff side of, 88
Naylor, Thomas Ellis, 53*n.*
Needham, Sir Christopher Thomas, 53*n.*
Nicolson, Harold, quoted, 107*n.*
Northcote, Sir Stafford, 25, 32, 33, 45, 80

OATMAN, Miriam E., 129*n.*, 143*n.*
Open competition, 42, 126, 175
Oral interview, 85, 88, 175
Order in Council of 1855, 39; of 1870, 42; of 1876, 46; of 1910, 6; of 1920, 6, 121
Ordnance, Board of, 32
Oxford and Asquith, Lord, quoted, 161, 170
Oxford, University of, 83, 86, 87, 102, 103, 109, 174; Union of, 68

PALMERSTON, Lord, 39, 71
P. and P. U. classes, 124
Parker, Charles Stuart, 38
Parliament, reform of, 2; scrutiny of orders by, 143
Parliament Act (1911), 3
Patronage system, 24, 26, 42
Peel, Sir Robert, 62, 71
Pensions. *See* Superannuation
Permanent heads of departments, 96
Personnel Classification Board, U. S., 95*n.*
Pitt, William, 18
Playfair, Lyon, 25, 45, 71
Playfair Commission, 45
Political speaking, 67
Pollock, James K., 112*n.*
Poor Law Board, 32

Post Office, 32, 116, 127
Pownall, Sir Assheton, 53*n.*
President's Committee on Administrative Management, 15*n.*, 80*n.*, 93
Price, Don K., 122*n.*
Primrose, Sir Henry, 52*n.*
Privy Council Office, 32
Promotion system, 107*n.*
Property qualifications, for voting, 18*ff.;* for membership in the House of Commons, 20
Provincial universities, 102
Public accounts committee, 122
Public Corporations, 6; salaries paid by, 150
Public schools, 61, 83, 103*ff.*
Pybus, Percy John, 53*n.*

RAMSAY, Sir Malcolm, 110
Redistribution Act, 19
Red tape, 151
Reeves, Floyd W., 80*n.*
Reform Act of 1832, 9, 18
Religious tests, for membership in the House of Commons, 20
Remuneration, of civil servants, 56; consolidation of, 56
Representation of the People Act (1918), 20
Richards, Robert, 53*n.*
Ridley, Sir Matthew White, 48
Roberts, H. A., 105*n.*
Robson, W. A., 144; quoted, 9, 102, 173
Rogers, Frederic, 28
Romilly, Edward, 25
Ronaldshay, Earl of, 171*n.*
Roosevelt, Franklin D., 77, 110*n.*
Rotation of office, 26
Rowse, A. L., quoted, 13
Rules Publication Act (1893), 142
Russell, Lord John, 38, 71

SALTER, Sir Arthur, quoted, 168
Sanders, C. A. W., 131
Sankey, Lord Chancellor, 138
Schechter case, 141
Schuman, Frederick L., quoted, 90*n.*
S. class, 125
Scott, Sir Leslie, 138
Scott, Sir Russell, 94, 106, 131
Second Division clerks, 49, 50
Sex Disqualification (Removal) Act (1919), 57

INDEX

Sharp, Henry, 53n.
Sharp, W. R., 106n., 166n.; quoted, 91, 93n., 129n.
Shipley, Arthur Everett, 52n.
Simon, Sir John, 163
Smellie, K. B., quoted, 8n., 23n., 152n.
Snowden, (Philip) Viscount, 52n., 71, 109, 130
Southborough, Lord, 124
Southwark, Bishop of, 52n.
Speaker's Conference, 19
Stamp, Sir Josiah, quoted, 80
Steed, Henry Wickham, quoted, 159
Stephen, Sir James, 25
Stephens, B. F., quoted, 78n.
Stephens, H. M., 36n.
Striking, right of, 51
Suffrage, issue of, 19; reform of, 19ff.; for women, 20
Superannuation, 57, 96
Supreme Court, U. S., 141, 142
Swift, Dean, on property qualifications, 21

Technical staffs, 56, 94; problems presented by, 51
Temporary Staffs committee, report of, 125n.
Thomas, J. H., 71, 74n.
Thring, Lord, 146n.
Times, The, 37
Tomlin, Lord, 53
Tomlin Commission. *See* Civil Service, Royal Commission on (1929-31)
Trade, Board of, 32, 160
Trade Disputes and Trade Unions Act (1927), 128, 130

Trade Union Congress, 128
Treasury, 31, 61
Treasury classes, 81
Treasury control, 6, 43, 44, 53, 120ff., 161
Treasury Interservice Committee, 8
Trevelyan, Sir Charles E., 25, 31, 32, 33, 80
Trevelyan, Sir George O., quoted, 36
Trollope, Anthony, 24
Typing classes, 123

Ullswater, Viscount, quoted, 22
University of London, 102, 174

Vansittart, Sir Robert, 173
Victoria, Queen, 37
Viva voce. *See* Oral interview

Walker, Harvey, 81n., 90
Wallas, Graham, 52n.
Wellesley, Lord, 35
Wellington, Duke of, 19
White, Leonard D., quoted, 107, 132, 133
Whitley Council system, 127, 130ff.
Willis, John, quoted, 140
Wilson, Sir Horace, 173
Wingfield-Stratford, Esmè, quoted, 17
Wintringham, Margaret, 53n.
Women civil servants, 53, 56, 57, 117
Woodgate, Sir Alfred E., 46
Works, Office of, 32
World War, effect on Civil Service, 117
Writing Assistants, 123

Augsburg College
George Sverdrup Library
Minneapolis, Minnesota 55404